D1505602

Traditional Yorkshire COOKING

with Mrs Simkins

More than 60 North Country recipes,
from Cinder Toffee to Yorkshire Moggy

Dalesman

Published in Great Britain in 2018 by Dalesman
an imprint of
Country Publications Ltd
The Gatehouse, Skipton Castle, Skipton BD23 1AL
www.dalesman.co.uk

Reprinted 2020

ISBN: 978-1-85568-375-4

Printed in China for Latitude Press Ltd.

CONTENTS

INTRODUCTION

Here's a collection of traditional Yorkshire recipes, stretching back down the generations, which have been given a bit of a makeover to suit modern tastes and kitchens.

The beautiful county of Yorkshire is like another country: geographically and economically huge with stunning scenery, bustling cities, a fine farming history and differing dialects, it's the largest county in England. No wonder it has such a plentiful supply of regional recipes — more than anywhere else in Britain.

All the recipes in this book are made from simple, homely ingredients, and many have quirky and unusual names: intriguing sorts of names to keep you guessing.

Yorkshire pudding is Yorkshire's most famous and well-loved dish. It's mentioned in records from the 1700s and no doubt it was around long before that. Early prototypes were known as dripping puddings and were cooked underneath the roast, which was more often mutton than beef as Yorkshire is sheep country. Naturally, it's been given a whole section to itself, with recipes and even poetry.

Parkin is another well-known Yorkshire recipe, dating back to Celtic times, along with its ancestors harcakes and tharf cakes, and more delicate cousin Yorkshire moggy.

Cinder toffee is very likely another Yorkshire original; and few people know that bonfire toffee, or Tom Trot as it's known locally, hails from Swaledale.

Read on and find out about other regional delicacies such as old wives' sod, nowt cake, tap-room loaf, Jordan cake, old wife's cake, Caddiston cake, growlers, scufflers and the like: the last two are more familiar than you think.

Mrs Simkins
June 2018

Ingredients
4oz butter or margarine
4oz sugar
3 eggs
2oz whole or ground almonds
9oz flour
4oz sultanas
1oz lemon peel
2oz glacé cherries
1 tablespoon golden syrup
1 teaspoon baking powder
2 tablespoons milk

Method. Cream the sugar and butter. Mix in the other ingredients gradually and add the milk to make to the consistency of a fruit cake. Add the baking powder last. Bake in a moderate oven for one and a half hours at Regulo 3 turning down to Regulo 2 after half an hour.

KIRBY HILL

CHERRY LOAF

Ingredients
5oz margarine or butter
5oz sugar
2 eggs
4oz cherries
10oz self raising flour
Milk to mix
A little sugar to sprinkle the top and a few cherries

Method. Cream the butter and sugar and add the eggs and cherr Cream well, then mix in the flour stirring in a little milk. mixture into greased loaf tin and sprinkle on cherries and su Bake in a moderate oven (350°F to 375°F) for one and a half ho

LONG RIS

CHERRY CAKE

Ingredients
¼lb butter
¼lb castor sugar
5 eggs
4oz glacé cherries
2oz ground almonds
1oz pistachio kernels
3oz candied peel
10oz flour
Half a nutmeg
Rind of a lemon
1 teaspoon baking powder

sugar to a cream. Add the eggs one at well between each one, and add the greased tin, eight inch square low oven.

MARTON-IN-CLEVELAND

CHOCOLATE B

Ingredients
3oz walnuts
2oz chocolate
3oz margarine
½ to
Pinc
Little

nd melt chocol
r fat and suga
lt, nuts and
ncy. Sprea
e top with a
Cut into

07

ACKNOWLEDGEMENTS

Sources:

Yorkshire Recipes, collected by Mrs Appleby, 1964 Dalesman Publishing

The Dalesman Book of Country Recipes, Kathleen Inglis, Dalesman readers and Anne R Burkett, 1983 Dalesman Publishing

Traditional North-Country Recipes, Joan Poulson, 1984, Cicerone Press

Yorkshire WI Recipe Book: Through Yorkshire's Kitchen Door, 1957, The Waverly Press

Also: The Foods of England website: http://www.foodsofengland.co.uk/

I'd also like to thank my Nana, Mrs Selina Hills, who was cook in a country house in Yorkshire before she married. Sadly no longer with us, she was an inspiring cook and the most lovely person generally.

Dalesman, *Down Your Way* and *Countryman* magazine readers may be familiar with some of these recipes, previously printed in monthly cookery columns: Mrs Simkins' Country Kitchen, Home Cooking with Mrs Simkins and Country Cooking with Mrs Simkins.

NETTLE **SOUP**

Nettles have been a traditional part of our spring diet for centuries. Before modern preserving methods, by late March, people were desperate for something green. Their constitutions weakened by a bleak wintry diet of starch and salted meat; they craved fresh, bitter tastes to perk up their palate and cleanse their systems. Nettle soups and potages, spring tansies and puddings were a popular way to eat wild greens.

Wear rubber gloves to pick and handle nettles before they're cooked when the sting becomes inactive. Harvest tender young tops from late March to the end of May.

Tip: you can also use dead nettle *Lamium album*, including garden varieties, to make soup in the same way.

1. Wash nettles and pick over. Remove thick stalks and chop finely.

2. Boil potatoes until tender in cold water to cover; drain: reserve water if using for stock.

3. Fry onion and carrot slowly until soft. Add garlic towards end of cooking time.

4. Add nettles and potatoes, season and stir to combine. Blend until smooth in food processor or blender. Return to washed pan and heat gently until piping hot.

5. Add 1-2 tablespoons cream before reheating or scatter with fried bacon lardons or croutons.

Note: if venturing further afield than your own garden, avoid plants polluted by busy roads, pesticides or livestock.

See also Easter ledges pudding, page 34

2 **handfuls young nettle tops**

4 **medium size potatoes, peeled & cubed**

400ml (just under ¾ pint) **vegetable stock***

1 **large onion, diced**

1 **carrot, peeled & grated (or finely diced)**

Knob of butter & 1 tablespoon **oil for frying**

1 **clove garlic, finely chopped**

A generous pinch ground mace

Coarsely ground black pepper, ground white pepper to taste

*alternatively dissolve ½ vegetable stock pot in 400ml of cooking water from the potatoes

SERVES 4

PEA POD SOUP

No self-respecting Yorkshire tyke or any other person from the north of England can abide waste. Home-grown peas from the allotment are a northern tradition, and much love and care goes into their growing. Who can bear to throw all the spent pea pods straight onto the compost heap whilst there is still so much goodness in them?

The full-size pods may be a little coarse and fibrous but they contain plenty of flavour and nourishment. Utilise them in a tasty stock for an easy version of the traditional pea pod soup.

Wash pea pods thoroughly before shelling when using for stock. The pods freeze easily too: make sure they are dry, and seal inside a freezer bag. Use for stock from frozen.

SERVES 4

500g (1lb 2oz) **clean pea pods, stalks removed, roughly chopped**

0.75-1 litre (2 pints) **hot water**

2 **medium-large potatoes, peeled and diced**

2 tablespoons **butter**

1 **onion, diced**

4-5 **spring onions, sliced**

1-2 **cloves garlic, finely chopped**

1 **vegetable gel stock pot**

Freshly ground black and ground white pepper to taste

1 Bring water to boil, add pods and simmer briskly for 5-8 minutes until tender but still bright green.

2 Transfer pods to blender or food processor with a slotted spoon, leaving cooking liquid in pan, and whiz to extract maximum flavour.

3 Strain pods, returning any liquid to pan. Discard pods. (Now they can go into the compost!)

4 Add diced potatoes to pea pod liquid and simmer briskly for 10 minutes or until soft. Add peas towards end of cooking time, cook for 3-5 minutes until tender.

5 Meanwhile, melt butter in another pan and cook onions slowly until soft and golden. Add garlic towards end, cook gently, then stir in gel stock pot.

6 Drain potatoes and peas, reserving liquid.

7 Transfer all vegetables to blender or food processor with a 1-2 ladleful of the cooking liquid and whiz smooth.

8 Return to washed pan, adjust seasoning, add more of the cooking liquid if required and heat until piping hot.

KIDDLY BROTH

Although this ancient broth is sometimes associated with Cornwall, forms of it are found everywhere and it was a typical mill workers' tea-time meal. No kidneys are involved: kiddly, or keddy, means kettle or pot, as it's made with hot water.

On a spectrum or sliding scale: at its lowest end, it was made with little but water and stale bread (toasted for extra flavour, if you were lucky). The next level would include onion, scant seasoning and ideally some bacon. Writer Thomas Hardy was a big fan down in Dorset.

At its most grim and basic, it's known as workhouse broth; but the absolute pinnacle would be the basic broth, with components fried in butter or dripping, and some good beef stock. Made this way, it's the perfect pick-me-up for getting back on your feet after an illness and is absolutely delicious.

1 large onion, diced

50g (2oz) bacon, diced (smoked lardons work well)

Splash of oil or knob of dripping

Approximately 100ml (2-3 fl oz) beef stock

600ml (1 pint) hot water

1-2 thick slices dry bread, cubed

Knob of butter or dripping

Ground white and coarsely ground black pepper

---

1   Fry onion and bacon slowly in oil or dripping. Add stock and pepper. Stir thoroughly.

2   Stir in water. Simmer for around 45 minutes. Fry bread in butter or dripping. Serve broth in warm bowls with bread on top.

3   Allow bread to sink into broth and soften – or eat immediately, according to preference.

OLD-FASHIONED
ONION TOASTS

The old ways are the best they say, and this simple dish has certainly stood the test of time: already an old recipe when it first appeared in the Farmhouse section of *The Dalesman Book of Country Recipes* published in 1983, it's as tasty and comforting as ever.

Here is the original recipe:

Spanish onions

Cheese

Hot buttered toast

Mustard

Salt and pepper

Fry some Spanish onions a nice brown and spread thickly over rounds of buttered toast.

Season. Cover with thin slices of cheese coated with a little mustard. Put into a hot oven or before a fire until the cheese is melted. Serve at once.

Little more needs to be said except to mention a white farmhouse loaf works well for the toast, cut into ½ inch slices. Season with a little pepper only (no need for any salt), slice the onions fairly thickly and cook slowly in half butter, half oil for best results.

In the absence of a hot fire, preheat oven to 200°C /180°C (fan oven) / Gas Mark 6 or equivalent. Set a rack on top of a baking tray to lay the toasts on and bake for around 10-15 minutes or until the cheese is bubbling. A piece of greaseproof paper on the tray will cut down on washing up.

PICKLED MUSHROOMS

This recipe originally appeared in the *The Dalesman Book of Country Recipes* published in 1983, as part of the first section: *Recipes from a Country Kitchen* by Kathleen Inglis.

Many recipes in this section were taken from Kathleen's grandfather's scrapbook. Her grandfather, William Bowdin, came from Hole Bottom Farm in Hebden. The family was musical, well known locally, and formed an orchestra. The mushrooms probably went down a treat with a snatched bread and cheese lunch during rehearsals.

Good with cold meats and salads, try adding them to stews and casseroles for a real flavour boost.

Rub mushrooms with flannel and salt

Here's the original recipe:

Pickled Mushrooms (Brown)

Rub small button mushrooms with a bit of flannel and salt. Throw a little salt over and put them in a stew-pan with some mace and pepper; as the liquor comes out shake them well and keep them over a gentle fire till all of it be dried into them again. Put as much vinegar into the pan as will cover them, give it one warm, and turn all into a glass or stone jar. They will keep two years and are delicious.

The recipe is so easy going: you can use any quantity of mushrooms to suit your jar size. Pack the jar with mushrooms first and allow about half as many again as they'll shrink during cooking.

Once you've measured the mushrooms, sterilize the jar with boiling water or wash on the hot cycle in the dishwasher.

Use a pan to accommodate the mushrooms in a single layer with a little 'shaking room'.

Follow the original recipe and keep a lid on the pan until the small amount of liquor starts to run.

If you're lucky, you'll have some spare spiced vinegar: use it to enhance stews and gravies.

TOASTED
WENSLEYDALE

*Served on a Muffin with Red
Onion & Mushroom*

Here's a new Yorkshire recipe. It's not unusual in the twenty-first century to visit a café or coffee shop in the hope of a nice toasted cheese sandwich for your lunch, and find yourself offered a variety of fancy paninis or 'toasted flatbreads' instead. Quite often, these are resplendent with a fashionable cheese that was never intended for toasting.

On the last occasion this happened to me, as I bit warily into a scorched pitta bread, I thought how much more successful a nice bit of Wensleydale on a toasted muffin would be.

So here you are, and much more tasty and satisfying it is too!

1. Slice the mushroom and onion: the slices should be nice and thin but not paper-thin.

2. Cook the mushrooms and onion in the oil over a moderate heat until soft but barely coloured: keep a lid on the pan for the first few minutes of cooking.

3. Drain on kitchen paper.

4. Split the muffin and lightly toast on both sides.

5. Heat the grill to its highest setting.

6. Pile the grated Wensleydale onto the muffin halves: there's no need to butter. Grind over a little black pepper.

7. Arrange the mushroom and onion slices generously on top of the cheese.

8. Grill until bubbling.

9. Serve immediately with a handful of salad leaves. A splash of Henderson's relish wouldn't go amiss either.

Per person:

1 **large chestnut mushroom**

½ **small red onion or equivalent**

Approximately ½ **tablespoon oil, rapeseed or similar**

1 **English muffin**

Approximately 40g (1½ oz) **Wensleydale cheese, coarsely grated**

Freshly ground black pepper

SERVES 4

WENSLEYDALE YORKSHIRE
TARTS

Here's another new Yorkshire recipe. Simple to make, the free-form, crisp, buttery pastry baked in a 4-cup Yorkshire pudding tin contrasts beautifully with the smooth Wensleydale filling.

Note: Wensleydale, thinly sliced or grated on the coarse side of a box grater tends to melt unevenly, which is great for toasted cheese. However, if you grate it on the fine side of the grater, it melts completely into the savoury custard giving a beautiful silky-smooth finish.

160g (5oz) **plain flour**

80g (2½oz) **butter, cold and cut into small pieces**

3 tablespoons **cold water**

Plus:

1 **medium onion finely diced**

1 tablespoon **oil**

1 **large egg**

6 tablespoons **double cream**

Large pinch dry mustard powder

Freshly ground black, ground white and cayenne pepper to taste

Good grating of nutmeg

50g (2oz) **Wensleydale, finely grated (on fine side of box grater)**

You will need a 4-cup Yorkshire pudding tin, plus baking beans and small squares of foil, cut to fit the tin

1   Preheat oven to 200°C /180°C (fan oven) / Gas Mark 6 or equivalent.

2   A food processor makes short work of the pastry.

3   Whiz flour and butter into fine crumbs. Add water and whiz until large clumps form.

4   Transfer to board and bring together with hands into a smooth ball. Divide in 4.

5   Roll each piece into a circle between ¼ and ½ centimetre thick. Drape each over a compartment, press gently into place and roll and pinch overhang into a rustic-style crust. Firm bottom edges gently with finger to seal.

6   Prick bottoms and cover with foil and baking beans. Bake for 15 minutes, remove foil and beans and bake for another 5-7 minutes.

7   Cool slightly. Reduce oven temperature to 160C (fan oven), gas mark 4.

8   Meanwhile, gently fry onion until soft and golden. Drain on kitchen paper.

9   Whisk egg and cream, stir in seasoning, Wensleydale and onion.

10 Pour into tart bases. Bake for 12-15 minutes or until filling puffed and golden.

11 Serve warm or cold.

YORKSHIRE **BRICK**

Here's a brand new 'traditional' recipe and I wouldn't be at all surprised if several other cooks around the county aren't coming up with something very similar.

Egg briks are one of the joys of North African travel: an egg with plenty of parsley sealed inside a triangular filo pastry parcel and deep fried. Try this homely baked version, cooked in a Yorkshire pudding tin. The combination of creamy, softly set egg, fresh parsley and crisp filo pastry is irresistible.

Give it an extra Yorkshire touch and serve with a spot of HP sauce or a shake of Henderson's Relish.

1   Preheat oven to 220ºC / 200ºC (fan oven) / Gas Mark 7 or equivalent.

2   Heat baking tray in oven.

3   Cut circles of greaseproof paper to fit bottoms of Yorkshire pudding cups. Brush cups and paper with melted butter.

4   Lay out your piece of filo pastry (the ½ sheet should result in a perfect square), brush top side with butter and drape over prepared cup.

5   Press gently into the sides of the cup with the tip of the brush bristles.

6   Crack in egg. Scatter with parsley, salt and pepper.

7   Bring the sides of the pastry over the egg, brushing with butter as you go.

8   Put the tin on top of the heated tray and bake for 8 minutes or until pastry is golden.

9   Serve immediately.

Per brick:

½ **standard sheet filo pastry**

1 **medium egg, fresh as possible**

Finely chopped parsley to taste

Salt & black & white pepper to taste

15g-20g (½-¾oz) **butter, melted**

Brown sauce or Hendo's, to serve

You will need a baking tray, 4-cup individual Yorkshire pudding tin, greaseproof paper and a pastry brush

YORKSHIRE
OLD WIVES' SOD

The name may sound forbidding and unappetising but this ages-old Yorkshire recipe still makes a quick and tasty lunch or supper. Surprisingly light and delicate when made with care it's also perfect if you're feeling poorly (or 'badly' as my nana used to say). If only we knew how it got its name!

3 **large eggs**

200ml (7½ fl oz) **semi-skimmed milk**

1 tablespoon **double cream**

Pepper, salt and butter

2-3 **oatcakes, lightly toasted and broken into pieces**

1   Preheat oven to 160ºC / 140ºC (fan oven) / Gas Mark 3 or equivalent

2   Beat eggs and stir in milk, Season and pour into a buttered baking dish approximately 800ml (1½ pints) capacity.

3   Scatter in oatcake pieces, dot with butter. Bake for 20-25 minutes or until golden and just set.

4   Eat immediately.

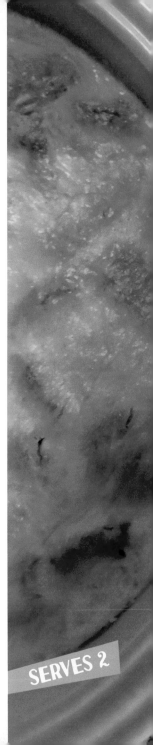

SERVES 2

YORKSHIRE **RAREBIT**

Usually associated with Wales, this glorious cheesy concoction on toast has been completely embraced by Yorkshire, adding its own variations. The naming of rarebits can be confusing. Here is the Yorkshire guide.

Rarebit or Rabbit?

There is some debate as to the meaning of the word rarebit and why it is sometimes changed to rabbit.

The dish, originally from Wales, may have come about because the Welsh are known to be especially fond of cheese, and historically, many a poor Welsh family was unable to afford meat.

Many families in other parts of Britain couldn't afford much meat either but were at least legally able to lay their hands on a rabbit 'for the pot'. Land laws peculiar to Wales made even this difficult for the Welsh.

Therefore, the Welsh were unlikely to have a rabbit or indeed a 'rare bit' of meat of any description therefore mainly ate cheese instead, resulting in the much-loved cheese delicacy that later migrated to Yorkshire.

100g (4oz) **mature Cheddar, grated**

2 tablespoons **milk**

1 **medium egg yolk**

Pinch of dry mustard

Good splash of Henderson's relish (or Worcester Sauce) and dash of Tabasco or shake of cayenne pepper

Plus:

4 **slices bread, not too thickly cut**

Butter for spreading

Note: with any rarebit, it's essential that the supporting toast is crisp: allow it to cool a little and let the steam escape before buttering very lightly, right to the edges.

The rarebit mix will store, covered, in the fridge for 2-3 days

Classic Rarebit

Cut into dainty squares or triangles or serve whole with salad for a knife-and-fork lunch. Crisp lettuce and tomato, coleslaw and oddly, orange segments, complement it beautifully.

1   Combine the cheese, egg yolk, milk and seasoning in a small heavy saucepan. Cook on a medium heat, stirring constantly. Once cheese has melted change to a whisk. Keep whisking and don't have the heat too high or the egg will split and scramble.

2   Once thick and smooth remove from heat and set aside; make the toast.

3   Spread the cheese mixture onto the toast and grill until bubbling and golden.

Buck Rarebit (or Golden Buck)

Classic rarebit topped with a poached egg.

Yorkshire Rarebit (also sometimes known as Golden Buck)

Definitions of Yorkshire rarebit vary but the determining factor is bacon: the basic rarebit mixture is grilled and topped with a couple of crisp rashers. A buck rarebit (or golden buck) is often used to describe a rarebit topped with a poached egg, but sometimes a Yorkshire rarebit is defined as a buck rarebit with bacon.

Venerable **Yorkshire Buck**

The venerable Yorkshire buck is a simplified variation cooked in the oven. Bread is spread with mustard and browned in a hot oven before being moistened with ale, topped with cheese and bacon and returned to the oven until the cheese is melted and the bacon crisp.

CARLIN PEAS

Not widely known outside the Midlands and the North, carlings or carlins are an ancient variety of dried pea. They make a tasty snack as the traditional 'parched peas' on Bonfire Night, with plenty of salt, pepper and vinegar.

Carlin Peas

Grown in Britain since the Middle Ages, the peas seem to have inexplicably fallen out of favour in more recent times. Nevertheless, twice a year, in parts of the North and Midlands they are still popular as traditional 'parched peas' on Carlin or Passion Sunday (the 5th Sunday of Lent) and Bonfire Night.

Also known as pigeon, maple, grey or black peas, or 'black badgers', they are not to be confused with the pigeon pea of Asian, African and Latin American cooking.

Nutty tasting and smooth skinned, they are equally good as a main meal or snack. Regular carlin fans will have their own family's way of preparing them. For the uninitiated, here are some basic guidelines.

Parched Peas

Sometimes sold in paper cups and served in bars on Carlin Sunday.

200g (7oz) dried carlin peas

Cold water to cover

Salt, pepper and vinegar to serve

1. Soak the carlins in approximately 1 litre (generous 2 pints) of water overnight.

2. Drain, rinse and boil for 40-45 minutes in a fresh litre / 2 pints of cold water. They should be cooked through but still with a pleasant yielding 'bite'.

3. Drain and serve hot with malt vinegar, salt and pepper. You may like to moisten them first with a little of the cooking water. They're also good cold.

Buttered Badgers

Boil and drain carlins as before. Fry for 3-5 minutes in salted butter, bacon fat or dripping. Season with pepper.

Bacon Badgers

Fry a chopped onion in oil slowly until soft. Add chopped bacon and brown lightly. Add boiled carlins, pepper and thyme leaves. Cook for 3-5 minutes. Serve with crusty bread or toast.

Variation: Any handy available greens can also be added for the last 3-5 minutes such as curly kale, rocket, sorrel or nettles.

WINDFALL APPLE
CHUTNEY

As you know, nobody living in the north of England likes to see anything go to waste. A Yorkshire friend and I came up with this recipe between us a while back. We both like our chutney with a bit of extra heat so scale down the spices if you prefer something milder.

We both agree slow cookers are ideal for making small batches of chutney*. It may take more than twice as long in cooking time but the whole process is very much simpler and more relaxed.

An extra bonus is that long, slow, cooking means the chutney comes out tasting beautifully mellow – as if it has already matured – so you can eat it straight away rather than waiting for the usual 2-3 months.

Use cooking apples, tart dessert, windfalls of either or a mixture. When using windfalls trim away any imperfections before adding to the pot and take this into account when weighing.

Mrs Simkins & Mr Whitley's
Apple Chutney
October '15

You will need an average 3-litre, 4-person slow cooker

Makes sufficient to fill 3 x average jam jars

2 **medium-large onions, chopped small**

1 kilo (just over 2lbs) **apples, peeled, cored and diced**

2 **garlic cloves, finely chopped**

Finely grated zest of 1 **orange (avoid long strands)**

450g (1lb) **dark brown sugar**

2 teaspoons **ground ginger**

1 teaspoon **ground cinnamon**

1 teaspoon **chilli flakes, or to taste**

150ml (¼ pint) **cider vinegar**

250g (9oz) **raisins, sultanas or a mixture of both**

¼ teaspoon **salt (optional)**

1   Mix the prepared onions and apples together in the slow cooker pot. Stir in the garlic, orange zest and sugar, and then the spices and vinegar.

2   Turn on the slow cooker and set to high.

3   Cook with the lid off, for 30 minutes.

4   Stir thoroughly and cook with the lid on until everything is bubbling and then wedge the lid partially open with a wooden spoon. Continue to cook for approximately 6 hours. Stir occasionally.

5   Add raisins/sultanas and salt (if using), and cook for around 2 hours with the lid off.

6   Once a trail made by drawing a spoon across the chutney no longer fills with liquid, stop cooking and transfer to hot, sterilised jars.

Note: if using old jars, it's advisable to buy new lids: vinegar corrodes damaged lids causing spoilage. Once opened, store chutney in fridge

*Firmer fruits and vegetables (apples, winter squashes) work well in a slow cooker, softer ones (marrows, plums) are less suitable.

MUM'S YORKSHIRE
PUDDING

The idea of Yorkshire pudding originally, was to eat it before the meat (not always beef) with plenty of gravy. Meat was, and still is, expensive so was served afterwards in small portions.

My mum taught me to make Yorkshire pudding although, funnily enough, she had been taught by my dad. Dad's mum, my nana, was ahead of her time and taught both her boys to cook. Naturally, it goes without saying, I have never been able to make a Yorkshire to top my mum's.

If you are from Yorkshire, you won't need this recipe at all so please ignore it and move on. If you are from out of the county and need a little help, here are some tips:

1. Both oven and cooking fat must be absolutely screaming hot.

2. The batter should be a) room temperature and b) the consistency of thin cream.

3. Never, ever, even think of opening the oven door whilst the pudding is cooking and for best results take it to the table the moment it's ready.

50g (2oz) **plain flour**

1 large egg, as fresh as possible

150ml (¼ pint) **semi-skimmed milk (for a slightly crispier pudding, you can use half milk, half water)**

Pinch of salt

Clarified beef dripping or lard, enough to coat bottom of tin thinly; alternatively, use oil such as rapeseed, vegetable, sunflower or corn

You will need a 20cm (8inch) fixed-bottom cake tin or similar, or a smallish roasting tin approximately 25 x 18cm (9 x 7inches), or a 4-cup Yorkshire pudding tin. An ordinary 12-cup tart tin works well for small individual puddings.

1. Preheat oven to 240°C / 220°C (fan oven) / Gas Mark 9 or equivalent.

2. Sieve flour into a roomy bowl.

3. Make a well in the middle and add the egg.

4. Stir it in with a dinner fork, incorporating all the flour from the sides.

5. Gradually add milk until you have a thin batter.

6. Add salt, change to a whisk and whisk thoroughly to incorporate more air into the mixture.

7. Leave to stand for 10-30 minutes at room temperature.

8. Add fat to tin and heat in hot oven until a slight haze rises from it.

9. Whisk batter briefly and pour into tin.

10. Bake for 20-30 minutes or 10 for individual ones until well risen, puffy and golden.

CLASSIC YORKSHIRE
PUDDING

The earliest recipe for Yorkshire Pudding as we know it, reproduced below, appeared in *The Art of Cookery Made Plain and Easy* by Hannah Glasse in 1747.

Take a Quart of Milk, four Eggs, and a little Salt, make it up into a thick Batter with flour, like a Pancake Batter. You must have a good Piece of Meat at the fire, take a Stew-pan and put some Dripping in, set it on the Fire, when it boils, pour in your Pudding, let it bake on the Fire till you think it is high enough, then turn a plate upside-down in the Dripping-pan, that the Dripping may not be blacked; set your Stew-pan on it under your Meat, and let the Dripping drop on the Pudding, and the Heat of the Fire come to it, to make it of a fine brown. When your Meat is done and set to Table, drain all the Fat from your Pudding, and set it on the Fire again to dry a little; then slide it as dry as you can into a Dish, melt some butter, and pour into a Cup, and set in the Middle of the Pudding. It is an exceeding good pudding, the Gravy of the Meat eats well with it.

Yorkshire Pudding Rules

By Ian McMillan

The tin must not gleam. Must never be new.
If there is dried sweat somewhere in its metal
It must be your mother's. The flour must be strong
And white as the face of Uncle Jack
When he came back from the desert. The eggs
Must come from an allotment. The allotment
Must belong to your father-in-law.
The eggs have to be broken
With one swift movement over the bowl.
If there is dried sweat somewhere in its Pyrex
It must be your mother's. The milk
Must have been delivered by Colin Leech
At 0430. The fork has to be an old one. The wrist
Must, simply must, ache after the mixing.
The flour must introduce itself to the yolk of the egg.
The egg has to be allowed to talk to the flour.
The milk must dance with them both: foxtrot, then quickstep.
The pepper must be scattered, black on off-white.
The oven has to be hotter than ever.
The lard has to come in a tight white pack.
The lard must almost catch fire in the oven.
The oven door must open and you must shout
JESUS CHRIST as the heat smacks you in the chops.

Follow these rules
And the puddings will rise to heaven
And far beyond.

EASTER LEDGES
PUDDING

*AKA dock or
passion pudding*

Puddings made with the first tender young leaves of spring and eaten as a tonic, are an old tradition. It was believed that the more bitter-tasting the leaves, the more effective they were at cleansing and purifying the system after winter.

New leaves of bistort or sweet dock, also called Easter ledges, are the main leaf in northern spring delicacy Easter ledges pudding, still popular today. Hebden Bridge in the Calder Valley holds a famous pudding competition every year on Passion Sunday, the fifth Sunday of Lent.

The mixture is sufficient to make 1x 2-pint pudding baked in the oven, or a dozen fried cakes

100g (4oz) **pearl barley, rinsed**

450ml (¾ pint) **vegetable stock**

1 **medium onion, diced**

5-6 **spring onions, sliced**

1-2 tablespoons **oil**

200g (7oz) **mix of bistort and other spring leaves, washed & finely chopped**

2 **medium eggs, beaten**

100g (4oz) **oatmeal**

1 rounded tablespoon **flour**

Ground white and freshly ground black pepper

1. Preheat oven to 180°C / 160°C (fan oven) / Gas Mark 4 or equivalent.

2. You will need a 1-litre (2-pint) pudding basins, the bottom lined with a circle of greaseproof paper.

3. Bring barley to the boil in the stock. Simmer 30 minutes or until soft.

4. Fry onions slowly until soft and sweet. Add greens and wilt. Remove from heat.

5. Drain barley, if necessary, add to pan. Stir in eggs, oatmeal, flour and pepper.

6. Transfer to basin. Smooth level. Cover with double thickness greaseproof paper, pleated to allow for expansion. Tie with string. Stand in roasting tin containing 2-3 cm (1 inch) warm water.

7. Bake 30-40 minutes until pale gold on top.

Tip: mix fresh new nettle tips, baby dandelion leaves, parsley, spinach, rocket and other spring leaves in with the bistort.

Easter Ledges Breakfast Cakes

Make mixture as before. If convenient whiz briefly in a food processor: this blends the flavours together beautifully and helps the cakes to hold their shape.

Mould into cakes and bake for 20-30 minutes in a preheated oven 200°C / 180°C (fan oven) / gas mark 6 or equivalent. Alternatively, shallow fry in hot oil or bacon fat on both sides for 5-10 minutes until piping hot and golden. Serve with bacon and fried eggs.

MAKES 8

SAVOURY DUCKS
AKA FAGGOTS

Faggots are one of those deliciously savoury and economical dishes that seem to have fallen out of favour. Once upon a time you could take a jug or bowl to your local butchers and get it filled with faggots or 'savoury ducks' swimming in steaming hot gravy. Unlike their distant Scottish cousin, haggis, which becomes more popular with every Burns' Night, faggots seem to have been unfairly passed over.

Butchers still sell faggots, but the gravy is long gone. If you have a mincer or food processor with a good strong blade, it's straightforward to make your own at home. Ask your butcher to sell you the various cuts of pig you'll need ready chopped, and a piece of pig's caul, otherwise known as caul fat, to hold them together and give the distinctive faggot finish.

Note: this recipe has a slightly lower proportion of liver than many butcher's faggots, giving a lighter texture and brighter flavour.

1. Preheat oven to 200°C / 180°C (fan oven) / gas mark 6 or equivalent.

2. If you are using a food processor, put everything in together and process until you have a thick, coarse paste.

3. Otherwise, mince the meats together in a hand mincer, transfer to a bowl and work in the other ingredients with a wooden spoon.

4. Take tablespoons of the mixture and shape with wet hands into 8 balls.

5. Wrap each ball in caul, overlapping to secure. Sit in the roasting dish join-side down. Cover with foil and bake for 1-1¼ hours until golden brown and sizzling. Remove foil for final 10-20 minutes.

6. Serve immediately, whilst the caul-encased outsides are still crispy, with mash and mushy peas and plenty of gravy. A shake of Hendo's wouldn't go amiss.

250g (9oz) **belly pork, rind removed**

100g (4oz) **fatty pork shoulder**

100g (4oz) **bacon pieces**

100g (4oz) **pig's liver**

100g (4oz) **bread crumbs**

1 **medium onion, finely chopped**

½ teaspoon **mace**

3-4 **sprigs curly parsley, finely chopped**

5-6 **small sage leaves, finely chopped**

Pinch chilli flakes

¼ teaspoon **salt**

Good shake of white pepper

Plus: pig's caul for wrapping

HOME-MADE GROWLERS

AKA hand-held pork pies

In parts of Yorkshire, small pork pies are called *growlers*. They are distinguished from cured pork pies elsewhere by a fractionally thinner, crunchier crust and the fact that they are eaten hot, liquefied jelly dribbling down the chin. The name refers to hand-held sizes: full-size pies are known as *stand pies*, which are eaten cold.

Growlers combine locally sourced meat and secret spice mixes. It's thought growlers may be so-called as they stop stomachs growling, and certainly a growler in the hand stops that sinking feeling. Mushy peas and mint sauce accompany growlers for sit-down meals.

It's not difficult to make your own pies, to eat hot or cold at home. Vary the seasoning to suit yourself and you'll soon have your own secret spice mix.

Chop pork finely by hand or use a food processor, take care not to over-process: the meat should be particulate, that is, in distinguishable pieces, not paste-like.

Ideally, pork-pie jelly is made from boiled pigs' trotters but it's not for the faint hearted; packet gelatine works well at home.

Tip: refrigerate overnight if eating cold as regular pork pies.

Filling
350g (¾lb) cubed lean pork shoulder (remove larger pieces of fat before weighing)

40g (1½oz) bacon lardons

½ -1 teaspoon ground white pepper

¼ teaspoon salt

½ teaspoon **each ground mace and dried sage**

Pastry
350g (¾lb) plain flour

½ teaspoon salt

½ teaspoon ground white pepper

100g (4oz) lard / vegetable shortening, diced

140ml (5 fl oz) water

1 small egg beaten with a teaspoon of water

Plus:

Sufficient powdered or leaf gelatine to make 300ml savoury jelly

300ml pork, chicken or vegetable stock

1   Pre-heat oven to 200°C / 180°C (fan oven) / Gas Mark 6 or equivalent.

2   You will need 4 greased 7cm ramekins and a baking tray, plus a small funnel for the jelly.

3   Process filling ingredients together briefly. Refrigerate.

4   Melt fat in a small saucepan with water and bring to the boil.

5   Sieve dry ingredients into a roomy bowl. Make a central well and stir in hot fat and water until combined. Transfer to a lightly floured board. Work into a pliable dough.

6   Divide into 4 equal pieces. Set aside quarter of each piece for lids. Shape main pieces into balls and roll into circles approximately ½ cm thick.

7   Line the ramekins, manoeuvring pastry gently into place. Use offcuts to repair any inadvertent tears. Trim away excess pastry, leaving sufficient to crimp together with the lid. Add trimmings to reserved lid pastry.

8   Roll out lids.

9   Divide filling into 4 and press into each pie; fill brimful.

10 Brush pastry edges with egg-wash. Position lids. Crimp together making a decorative edge. (Avoid overhang or pies will be difficult to un-mould.) Make small central holes in each lid. Brush lids with egg-wash.

11 Bake for 30 minutes. Remove from oven, cool briefly. Remove from ramekins. Position on baking tray, brush sides with egg wash, cover tops with greaseproof paper. Return to oven for 20 minutes until sides are golden brown. Cool slightly.

12 Make gelatine according to maker's instructions with stock. Pour gradually through small funnel into lid holes.

HASLET

Growing up over the border in Lincoln, haslet
was the savoury mainstay of many a high tea
or lunchtime sandwich in our house. It's a
traditional Lincolnshire 'baked meat' speciality.
It is pronounced 'hacelet' in and around the
county, although whenever it pops up elsewhere
in the country it's usually called 'hazlet'.

Pig farming has a long history in Lincolnshire. Among other crops, the rich
fenland produces exactly the kind of food pigs love: cereal and potatoes.

Sage, also plentiful in Lincolnshire, is a traditional flavouring for local pork
products: haslet, Lincolnshire sausages and pork pies. Its distinctive taste
complements pork beautifully and its antimicrobial properties preserve the meat.

You can eat it hot but we always had it cold: thinly sliced with a salad and pickles,
mustard or brown sauce, and in sandwiches.

Pig's Caul Membrane

You can bake haslet in a small loaf tin but for very best results you will need a length of pig's caul fat (or lace fat) membrane to wrap round it. This holds the haslet together, bastes it as it cooks and provides the distinctive outer layer.

Ask your local butcher for a piece: it's wise to give several days' notice as the membrane covers the pig's entire intestines and although it's very lengthy there is only one per pig.

An ordinary food processor is the perfect machine for home haslet production. The bread, brown or white, should be a day or two old – but not completely dry – and ideally proper baker's bread rather than from a sliced loaf.

1   Preheat oven to 200°C / 180°C (fan oven) / gas mark 6 or equivalent.

2   Tear the bread into pieces and process into crumbs: they needn't be too fine.

3   Add the pork, onion and seasoning.

4   Process until the mixture is the texture of sausage meat and is clumping together on one side of the processor bowl.

5   Shape the mixture into a rounded loaf and wrap in a piece of membrane to cover it completely: tuck it underneath and cut away any excess with sharp kitchen scissors.

6   Bake in an oven dish for 50 minutes to an hour, until brown on top, sizzling and completely cooked through.

Makes 1 standard size haslet

500g (1lb) **lean pork mince**

½ **smallish onion, finely chopped**

1 teaspoon **salt**

1 teaspoon **ground white pepper**

1 generous teaspoon **dried sage**

225g (8oz) **bread (both crumb and crust)**

Piece of pig's caul fat membrane, to cover (see above)

SERVES 4–5

MEAT AND TATIE PIE

Typical heartening northern England food, this popular pie is just the thing to come home to during the dark days of winter. Many versions incorporate potatoes within the filling but best of all is a layer on top, underneath the pastry. Henderson's Relish (Sheffield's own unique version of Worcestershire sauce, and incidentally, voted one of the top 75 great icons of Yorkshire by *Dalesman* magazine readers in 2016) adds extra depth of flavour.

We used to have similar version with the potatoes tucked up under the pastry lid for school dinners. To be honest, the main courses weren't always up to much, and that's putting it mildly, but the school did this nicely and I've continued the tradition.

1 You will need a 24cm / 9 inch pie dish and a food processor.

2 Fry onion until soft. Remove and keep warm.

3 Toss steak in flour. Fry in batches until browned. Remove and keep warm.

4 Combine relish, treacle and water and pour into pan slowly, stirring throughout and scraping up any cooked-on residue. Return onions and steak to pan and add pepper.

5 Bring to the boil, stirring frequently. Lower heat and simmer for 2 hours until meat is tender (or continue in a slow cooker for several hours).

6 Transfer to pie dish, reserving any surplus gravy, and cool slightly. Slice potatoes thickly and arrange over top. Grease rim.

7 For the pastry: whiz flour and butter into crumbs in processor. Add water. Whiz until large clumps form. Remove from machine and form into a ball.

8 Roll to the thickness of a pound coin. Cut out pie lid and lift onto dish leaving any over-hang. Firm edges gently with a fork or a knife handle.

9 Brush lightly with egg-wash. Make central hole.

10 Bake for 30 minutes in a preheated oven at 200°C / 180°C (fan oven) / gas mark 6 or equivalent, or until golden brown. Trim overhang with a sharp knife.

11 Serve with mashed potatoes, mushy peas, spare gravy and a shake of Hendo's.

Filling

1 medium onion, chopped

2 tablespoons oil

450g (1lb) braising steak, trimmed and cubed

1 tablespoon plain flour

1 tablespoon Henderson's relish

1 teaspoon black treacle

300ml (½ pint) hot water

Ground white pepper to taste

Roughly 400g (14oz) cold boiled potatoes (pre-cooked weight)

Pastry

220g plain flour

110g cold salted butter, diced

3½ tablespoons cold water

1 small egg beaten with 1 teaspoon water

MRS APPLEBY'S MEAT ROCK CAKES

Mrs Appleby was for many years the cookery columnist of the *Dalesman*. She travelled all over the Dales collecting and recording recipes from local people. Although the following recipe adapted from her book *Yorkshire Recipes*, published in 1964, sounds distinctly uninspiring, it's actually very tasty and something a bit different to make with your Sunday roast leftovers.

Makes 6 cakes

110g (2oz) **flour**

225g (½lb) **cooked lean meat, minced or finely chopped**

1 **medium onion, finely diced**

25g (1oz) **suet**

Freshly ground black and ground white pepper, to taste

Salt to taste, if required

1-2 tablespoons **gravy (or stock) to mix**

1. Preheat oven to 200oC / 180oC (fan oven) / gas mark 6 or equivalent.

2. You will need a greased baking tray.

3. Mix all ingredients together, seasoning well. Moisten with gravy to consistency of rock cakes mixture.

4. Divide into 8 with wet hands and heap into fairly shallow, rock cake-style piles on baking tray. Bake for 20-30 minutes until brown on top and piping hot inside.

5. Serve with vegetables, mashed potatoes and gravy, or baked potatoes and salad.

Collected by
M^RS. APPLE[B]
of the 'DALESM[AN]

SERVES 3-4

Rock cakes are a popular British individual currant cake or bun in which the dough is piled free-form on the baking tray to create a rough, rocky surface. *See also Drunken scoundrels, page 70*

PAN HAGGERTY

This traditional potato dish can be traced back mainly to the northern counties of England: Lancashire, Yorkshire, Cumbria, Durham and Northumberland.

Originally, pan haggerty was made on the hob in a single pan which was then taken to the table. If the household budget didn't run to plates, everybody could help themselves straight from the pan.

Some say the name may originally have come from the Old English word for the cooking pan itself: *panhin*. Haggerty may also be something to do with the ragged hash-like look of the finished dish.

For tastiest results, pre-cook the potatoes and onions as follows and bake in the oven instead.

700-800g (1½lbs) cold boiled potatoes sliced, not too thinly	**1** Preheat oven to 200°C / 180°C (fan oven) / gas mark 6 or equivalent.
1 large onion, sliced	**2** You will need a buttered oven-proof dish.
1-2 tablespoons **vegetable oil**	**3** Fry onion slowly until soft and turning golden.
Freshly ground black and ground white pepper and a little salt	**4** Arrange half the potatoes in the dish, season and spread onions over.
	5 Cover with remaining potatoes and season again.
Around 50g (2oz) **grated cheese**	**6** Bake for 15 minutes, remove from oven and scatter with cheese. Return to oven for a further 10-15 minutes. Serve immediatel

SERVES 2–4

SODA WATER
MEATBALLS

The inspiration for this recipe comes from *The Dalesman Book of Country Recipes* published in 1983. Bicarbonate of soda dissolved in water is sometimes used to help meatballs stay moist and tender, particularly in American recipes. The *Dalesman* version uses soda water (or club soda as it's called in America) instead.

Apparently, the protein molecules in meat can seize up in hot temperatures and the soda changes the PH level of the protein so it can be cooked at high heat without developing a rubbery texture. Whatever the scientific reason, the meatballs certainly taste good: bacon is included instead of the more usual pork, adding another layer of flavour.

Equally good served with mashed potatoes, vegetables and gravy, or tomato sauce and spaghetti with grated cheese on top.

MAKES 16

1. Combine all ingredients except soda water in a large bowl and work with your hands until thoroughly mixed. Gradually work in the soda water.

2. Divide the mixture into 16 and shape into balls.

3. Chill for at least 30 minutes.

4. Bake in a preheated oven at 200°C / 180°C (fan oven) / gas mark 6 or equivalent for 25-30 minutes until sizzling and golden brown. Turn over half way.

5. Alternatively, fry the meatballs in a small amount of oil.

Tip: play around with the seasoning to suit yourself; finely chopped parsley or thyme work well, or you may like some garlic. Increase or leave out chilli if you prefer.

450g (1lb) **lean beef mince**

125g (5oz) **streaky bacon, smoked or unsmoked, diced**

1 **smallish onion, diced**

100g (4oz) **fresh white breadcrumbs**

Small red chilli (or to taste) finely chopped

¼ teaspoon **mustard powder**

¼ teaspoon **salt (or to taste)**

Ground white and freshly ground black pepper to taste

50ml (2 fl oz) **soda water**

LAMMAS LOAF

Lammas or loaf-mass is on 1st August, which is also Yorkshire Day. Traditionally, loaves of bread, baked with fine flour from the year's first grain harvest, were taken to church as a thanksgiving.

Lammas is still celebrated in churches today, on the nearest Sunday to 1st August. Communion wafers are sometimes replaced by a loaf baked by one of the congregation and shared among the communicants. Intricate wheat sheaf-shaped loaves might be on display, particularly in country parishes.

Incidentally, if you are thinking of taking a loaf to your local church, don't dust it over-liberally with flour: even the most kindly vicar can cut up a bit rough when faced with flour all over the altar cloth!

450g (1lb) **strong white bread flour**

1 teaspoon **salt**

1 teaspoon **sugar**

1 teaspoon **easy bake yeast**

300ml (½) pint **warm water**

1 tablespoon **vegetable or rapeseed oil**

You will need a baking tray lined with greaseproof paper (or use a greased 18cm (9inch) loose bottomed cake tin for an appealing cake-shaped loaf)

1. Combine flour, salt, sugar and yeast in a roomy bowl. Using the fingertips of one hand, incorporate water and oil. Knead dough vigorously with both hands for 10-20 minutes, pulling, stretching and folding to develop the gluten, until smooth and silky.

   (If you have a bread machine, make a similar amount of dough before following the recipe from here.)

2. Leave to prove until virtually doubled in size.

3. Turn onto a lightly floured board, knead again briefly. Transfer to the tray and mound, into a bun shape and leave to rise again as before.

4. Bake in a preheated oven (200–220°C / 180–200°C (fan) / Gas Mark 6–7 or equivalent) for approximately 20 minutes or until golden brown.

5. Transfer to a wire rack to cool. A clean tea towel will keep it moist as it cools.

Tips

Be sure the dough has risen sufficiently before it goes into the oven.

You may like to score a traditional cross in the top just before baking: hold the knife vertically and cut approximately 1cm deep.

PIKELETS

A pikelet is like a flatter, free-form crumpet. Some say they originated in the Midlands, others say definitely the North of England. As welcome on a chilly summer day as in the depths of winter: serve hot from the pan thickly buttered, with or without jam, or toast later. These pikelets are raised the old-fashioned way with yeast.

1   You will need a small ladle (holding around 25ml) and a large flat-base frying pan.

2   Combine flour, yeast and salt in a roomy bowl. Mix thoroughly.

3   Stir in milk and water. Whisk well.

4   Cover bowl with clean tea towel and set aside for up to 3 hours until bubbling and active.

5   Heat pan until moderately hot. (Not too hot, turn down heat later if necessary.)

6   Add small amount of oil and butter and, once sizzling, add ladlefuls of batter, spacing out well: cook no more than 3 or 4 pikelets at a time.

7   Leave to cook for 4-5 minutes without disturbing: once tops look dull and dry, turn carefully and cook top side for around 1 minute until golden.

Pikelets are identical to Welsh crempog. Crempog are often served in a stack, oozing with butter and syrup, and cut into wedges as a birthday treat.

250g (9oz) **strong bread flour**

¾ teaspoon **easy-bake dried yeast**

1 teaspoon **salt**

175ml (6 fl oz) **warm milk and** 175ml (6 fl oz) **warm water combined**

Plus butter and oil for frying

MAKES AROUND 18

SCUFFLERS

Identification and naming of bread rolls can be a bit of a minefield in Britain. Depending on where you are in the country, you could be tucking into a bap or a barm, a teacake or bread cake, a stottie or a cob or even a softie if you are in Aberdeen. Most are unique in some way, differing slightly in shape, size, method of baking, texture and so on.

There are many more names to choose from but perhaps the most endearingly named bread roll of all is the scuffler from the Castleford area of Yorkshire. Triangular in shape and light in texture, the top is always dusted with flour.

This easy home version makes 8 soft-textured, dusty little scufflers.

1 Combine flour, salt, sugar and yeast in a roomy bowl. Make a central well and gradually mix in water and oil. Knead into a ball and transfer to a lightly floured work surface.

2 Knead dough vigorously for around 10 minutes until silky smooth.

3 Leave in a warm place for a couple of hours until virtually doubled.

4 Knead again briefly, mould into 2 equal rounds. Cut large cross in top of each so they will pull easily into four and prove again for 1-2 hours.

5 Dust with flour and bake in a preheated oven: 200-220°C / 180-200°C (fan oven) / Gas Mark 6-7 or equivalent for approximately 25-30 minutes until golden brown and bottoms sound hollow when tapped.

See also Yorkshire Teacakes, page 60

500g **strong white bread flour**

1 teaspoon **salt**

1 tablespoon **sugar**

1½ teaspoons **easy-bake yeast**

330ml **tepid water**

2 tablespoons **mild oil**

You will need 2 large greased baking trays

CHRISTMAS
TAP-ROOM LOAF

A slice of this deliciously moist and spicy fruit loaf is equally good plain or buttered with either a cup of tea or a glass of ale. It's also perfect with a slice of crumbly Wensleydale or mature Cheddar.

Also called spiced bread, based on an original recipe from the *Yorkshire WI Recipe Book* (1957) and sent in by the Moss and Fenwick branch, this was served every Christmas in the tap room of a local coaching inn, together with the traditional house Christmas ale.

Makes 3 1lb (500g) loaves (or 1 2lb (1000g) and 1 1lb (500g))

500g (1lb 2oz) **plain flour**

1 teaspoon **mixed spice**

½ teaspoon **ground ginger**

Generous grating of whole nutmeg

1 level teaspoon **baking powder**

¼ teaspoon **salt**

250g (8oz) **butter, diced**

250g (8oz) **soft light brown sugar**

¾ teaspoon **easy-bake dried yeast**

750g (1lb 7oz) **mixed dried fruit and peel**

2 medium eggs beaten into 300ml (½ pint) liquid made up of half milk and half water

You will need 3 greased 1lb loaf tins, the bottom lined with greaseproof paper (or 1 2lb tin and 1 1lb tin)

1 Preheat oven to 170°C / 150°C (fan oven) / Gas Mark 3 or equivalent.

2 Combine flour, spices and baking powder in a large bowl. Rub in butter until fine crumbs form. Add sugar and yeast and mix in thoroughly with hands in quick, light movements.

3 Mix in dried fruit and stir in liquid.

4 Divide between tins and bake for 1¼ hours or until golden, springy to the touch, and a skewer inserted comes out clean.

5 Allow to settle for 10 minutes before turning out. Cool on a wire rack.

Note: provided tins are filled to the same depth, baking times for larger and smaller tins are the same.

YORKSHIRE
BARM BRACK

Who doesn't enjoy a slice of barm brack with their tea? Plain or buttered, it's always welcome. Uncomplicated to make, you can vary the type of brown sugar, fruit and spices to suit yourself and what's in the cupboard. There's no fat in the recipe itself: useful if you are on a special diet.

Should you add a drop o' summat to your brack? "A drop o' summat good" as my nana used to say? The suggested couple of spoonfuls of whisky deepens the flavour and gives a cheering lift for special occasions but use milk or extra tea if you prefer.

Barm brack or barmbrack was originally raised with yeast or 'barm' acquired in jugs from the local brewery. Traditionally Yorkshire, similar types are also a staple in other parts of the country, including Northern Ireland and Wales.

Usually made in a loaf tin by modern bakers, a round cake makes an appealing change, echoing the early days when the yeasted brack was shaped by hand into a round.

1. Preheat oven to 180°C / 160°C (fan oven) / Gas Mark 4 or equivalent.

2. You will need a buttered round, deep, cake tin or silicone mould, or buttered lined 500g (1lb) loaf tin.

3. Soak dried fruit and sugar in tea overnight: keep it covered.

4. Combine flour and raising agents and sieve half over mixture. Add egg and stir in, gradually incorporating remaining flour and the spices.

5. Mix in whisky, milk or extra tea and ease into prepared tin. Smooth top with back of a tablespoon dipped in water.

6. Bake for 50-60 minutes until a skewer inserted comes out clean. Brush top with melted butter whilst still warm. Barm brack goes down a treat with a wedge of Wensleydale.

Tip: if using a silicone mould, cool cake completely before turning out.

500g (1lb) mixed dried fruit and peel

150ml (¼ pint) hot tea

75g dark brown sugar

225g (8oz) plain flour plus 1½ teaspoons baking powder (or use self-raising flour)

1 large egg

1 teaspoon mixed spice

½ teaspoon ground ginger

Generous grating of nutmeg

2 tablespoons of whisky (or milk, or more tea, warm or cold)

Melted butter for finishing

YORKSHIRE TEA CAKES

The main recipe is for a fruited or currant tea cake as eaten split and toasted up and down the country, but in parts of Yorkshire – the West Riding and Barnsley in particular – and some areas of Lancashire and Cumbria, a teacake can also mean a sizeable flat plain roll not unlike a bap.

Plain Tea Cakes

If you would like to make plain ones, make as for main recipes but reduce sugar to half a teaspoon and leave out fruit. You can also replace some of the white flour with wholemeal or granary.

You can buy teacakes ready filled in bakeries and cafés for lunch or mid-morning snacks.

A popular way to eat a plain tea cake at home is split, toasted, buttered and spread thinly with Marmite – sometimes cut into fingers for children and the delicately inclined.

You will need a greased baking tray

500g strong bread flour (1lb 2oz)

1 level teaspoon salt

35ml (1½ fl oz) rapeseed/vegetable oil (or 35g lard or block vegetable shortening, diced, if you prefer)

1 level tablespoon **sugar**

1 teaspoon **easy bake yeast**

175g (6oz) **mixed dried fruit and peel**

300ml (½ pint) **warm water**

Plus melted butter for finishing

1. Combine flour and salt into a roomy bowl. If using lard / shortening rub in now.

2. Stir in sugar, yeast and dried fruit.

3. Make a central well and pour in water and oil. Stir thoroughly.

4. Once mixed, work the dough with your hands into a cohesive ball that comes away cleanly from the bowl.

5. Transfer to a work surface and knead vigorously for 10-15 minutes until smooth and silky. Dust surface lightly with flour if necessary.

6. Leave in a clean bowl, covered with a damp tea towel for an 1-3 hours until virtually doubled in size.

7. Once sufficiently risen, knead once more, briefly this time, and divide into 8 equal pieces.

8. Mould into balls: roll each piece between cupped hands and flatten into rounds. Space out on tray and leave to rise again until almost doubled in size.

9. Bake in a preheated oven at 200°C / 180°C (fan oven) / gas mark 6 or equivalent for 20-25 minutes until golden brown.

10. Brush tops with melted butter whilst warm then cool on a wire rack.

CUTS INTO 16 SQUARES

APPLE SHORTCAKE

On a nippy autumn day there's nothing like settling down at the kitchen table with a piece of warm apple shortcake, fresh from the oven, and a pot of tea.

Tip: you can also use dessert apples but omit sugar. If using a combination, adjust sugar accordingly.

Pastry

250g (9oz) **plain flour**

2 level teaspoons **baking powder**

75g (3oz) **butter, diced**

75g (3oz) **golden caster sugar, plus more for finishing**

1 medium **egg, beaten**

4 tablespoons **milk**

1-2 teaspoons **cinnamon**

Filling

700g (1½lbs) **Bramley apples**

1 tablespoon **lemon juice**

75g (3oz) **granulated sugar (or 100g / 4oz if you have a sweet tooth)**

3 tablespoons **water**

---

1   Preheat oven to 200°C / 180°C (fan oven) / gas mark 6 or equivalent.

2   You will need a lightly buttered 20cm (8 inch) brownie tin or similar, the bottom lined with greaseproof paper.

3   Peel and core apples and cut into smallish even-size chunks. Toss in lemon juice as you go, to prevent browning and for extra zesty flavour. Set aside.

4   Cook apples gently with sugar and water for 5-10 minutes or until just tender. Strain off juice.

5   Sift flour and baking powder into a bowl. Rub in butter, stir in sugar and make a well in the centre.

6   Combine egg and milk and pour into dry ingredients. Gradually incorporate dry ingredients into wet with a wooden spoon, then bring the mixture together with your hands.

7   Gently knead into a smooth ball. Divide into 2 equal pieces.

8   Roll first piece gently into a rough rectangle the same size as tin and press lightly over the bottom to make the base.

9   Lay apple over mix and sprinkle with cinnamon.

10   Roll out second piece of dough and cover apples: don't worry if the soft dough looks a little torn and patchy, it's meant to look homely, and over-handling can toughen the finished texture.

11   Sprinkle with more sugar and bake approximately 20 minutes until risen and golden.

12   Serve warm or cold.

BACHELOR CAKE

Fruit cakes are always popular in Yorkshire and this is an old northern recipe, thought to be a good cake for a young girl to bake to impress her betrothed, something to show off her competent 'plain cooking' skills.

Any single chap would be pleased to receive one: it's handy to keep in the cupboard for those peckish moments and goes very well with a wedge of cheese.

The original recipe was mixed with just milk. For even better eating quality and bachelor-impact, I've slipped in a couple of eggs.

1. Preheat oven to 140°C / 150°C (fan oven) / Gas Mark 3 or equivalent.

2. You will need a greased 23cm (9in) loose bottomed cake tin or silicone mould.

3. Sieve flour, baking powder and spices into a bowl. Rub in butter until texture of breadcrumbs. Stir in sugar.

4. Add marmalade and fruit to mixture and stir to combine. Gradually stir in eggs and milk.

5. Stir thoroughly and transfer to the tin.

6. Bake for 50-60 minutes or until golden brown and a skewer inserted comes out clean.

7. If using a silicone mould, allow to cool completely before turning out.

Tip: for a nice sheen, brush cake with melted butter whilst still warm. Sprinkle with sugar as well if you like.

340g (12oz) **plain flour**

2 teaspoons **baking powder**

1 teaspoon **each: mixed spice, cinnamon, ginger**

75g (3oz) **salted butter, diced**

50g (2oz) **sugar – golden granulated works well**

2 tablespoons **marmalade**

500g (1lb) **dried fruit – mixed fruit with peel, raisins or whatever's available**

2 **large eggs, beaten, made up to** 300ml (½ pint) **with milk**

CADDISTON **CAKE**

There's something about this old-fashioned light fruit cake, with its moist crumbly texture and hint of citrus, that keeps you coming back for more. The ingredients are added in a particular and slightly unusual order. Maybe that's why: the secret's in the mixing!

The original recipe comes from the 1957 version of the *Yorkshire WI Recipe Book*, subtitled *Through Yorkshire's Kitchen Door*, contributed by the Kirby Hall branch. (Baking times have been adjusted for more modern ovens.)

110g (4oz) **butter**

110g (4oz) **caster sugar (or 75g (3oz) if you prefer a less sweet cake)**

3 **medium eggs**

50g (2oz) **ground almonds**

250g (9oz) **plain flour**

110g (4oz) **sultanas**

25g (1oz) **mixed peel**

50g (2oz) **glacé cherries**

1 tablespoon **golden syrup**

1 level teaspoon **baking powder**

2 tablespoons **milk, room temperature**

1. Preheat oven to 160°C / 140°C (fan oven) / Gas Mark 3 or equivalent.

2. You will need a greased 23cm (9in) cake tin.

3. Cream together butter and sugar. Stir in remaining ingredients in order.

4. Bake for 45-50 minutes until a skewer inserted comes out clean.

Method Notes

Soften the butter before mixing: golden caster sugar works well.

If you prefer, cream butter and sugar, and then add ingredients, one at a time, as far as and including, the flour, in a food processor. Beat each egg separately and add gradually through the processor spout with the motor running. Add almonds and flour gradually the same way: put them in a jug if it's easier.

Scrape the mixture into a bowl and continue as directed. Quarter cherries and dust in a little flour before adding.

COURTING CAKE

There are differing views as to what constitutes a courting cake, but most people agree it's a sponge cake filled with cream and strawberries, baked by a young woman to give to a young man she has her eye on. It's the sort of cake to turn a lad's head: some say if a lad accepts a cake from a lass they are as good as engaged!

An electric hand-held or stand mixer is helpful: use the beater attachment. This large cake cuts into 8–12 slices.

225g (8oz) **salted butter, softened**

225g (8oz) **golden caster sugar**

350g (12oz) **plain flour**

3 level teaspoons **cream of tartar**

1½ teaspoons **bicarbonate of soda**

4 **medium–large eggs, as fresh as possible**

4 tablespoons **milk**

1-2 tablespoons **sieved raspberry jam (optional)**

Around 500g (1lb) **strawberries**

300g (10½ fl oz) **double cream, whipped into soft peaks**

1 Preheat oven to 180°C / 160°C (fan oven) / Gas Mark 4 or equivalent.

2 You will need 2 greased 20cm (8in) loose-bottomed sandwich tins.

3 Cream butter and sugar together until light and fluffy.

4 Combine flour and raising agents: sieve half over mix, and add eggs and remaining flour.

5 Mix to combine, add milk and mix until smooth and glossy.

6 Pour into prepared tins.

7 Bake for 25-30 minutes or until risen and golden and a skewer inserted comes out clean.

8 Cool, spread each cake thinly with jam, if using, top with sliced strawberries and cream and stack one on top of the other just before serving.

Light Buttercream Alternative

Here's a handy alternative to fresh cream that complements the fruit beautifully. The cake can be assembled further ahead: buttercream holds its shape longer than fresh and is less perishable.

110g (4oz) salted butter, softened   **225g (8oz) icing sugar, sieved**

¼ teaspoon vanilla extract   **2-3 tablespoons lemon juice**

Beat butter until creamy in a roomy bowl. Add icing sugar, a little at a time and stir vigorously to combine. Finally, stir in vanilla and lemon juice to loosen mixture to spreadable consistency.

Note: slightly bruised strawberries are traditional: perhaps this symbolises the possibility that the young lady bakers suffered heartache in the past?

DRUNKEN SCOUNDRELS

Similar to a festive rock cake or bun, this seasonal variation of the old Yorkshire favourite Fat Rascals has a distinctly merry flavour: perfect for Christmastide. Serve warm or cold with a pot of tea or something stronger.

1   Preheat oven to 220°C / 200°C (fan oven) / Gas Mark 7 or equivalent.

2   You will need a greased baking sheet.

3   Soak the fruit in the sherry overnight.

4   Add the raising agents and spice to the flour and sieve into a roomy bowl.

5   Rub in the butter. Stir in the sugar and then the strained fruit, reserving the soaking sherry. Combine the sherry with the egg and milk and stir in gradually.

6   Use a dessertspoon to space out nine mounds of mixture on the prepared tray.

7   There's no need to make them too uniform: they should look a bit dishevelled.

8   Bake for around 12-15 minutes or until golden brown and a skewer inserted comes out clean.

Don't over-bake: they should be light and moist inside and a little bit crisp around the outside.

50g (2oz) **mixed dried fruit and peel**

50ml (1¾ fl oz) **sherry**

220g (8oz) **plain flour**

2 level teaspoons **cream of tartar**

1 level teaspoon **bicarbonate of soda**

½ teaspoon **mixed spice**

110g (4oz) **salted butter, softened**

40g (1½ oz) **golden caster sugar, plus extra for finishing**

1 **large egg, beaten**

50ml (1¾ fl oz) **milk at room temperature**

9 **glacé cherries (the red, gold and green ones add a nice touch)**

JORDAN CAKE

Here's a real old Yorkshire favourite from years ago, that appeared at many a church festival or gathering. A no-nonsense, practical plain cake, it was baked in a low oven, sometimes coming out with a slightly speckled top. It was often made in a meat tin and cut into squares.

Originally plenty of elbow grease was involved in the creaming and mixing but today a food processor makes it all quick and easy.

Cuts into 16 squares

50g (2oz) **salted butter, softened**

110g (4oz) **sugar – caster sugar works well**

175g (6oz) **plain flour**

1 level teaspoon **baking powder**

2 **medium–large eggs, beaten**

3 tablespoons **milk**

1   Preheat oven to 160°C / 140°C (fan oven) / Gas Mark 3 or equivalent.

2   You will need a 20cm (8in) greased brownie tin with the bottom lined with greaseproof paper, cut to fit.

3   Whiz the butter and sugar together in a food processor. Combine the flour and baking powder and sieve over the top, covering it completely. Add the eggs and milk and whiz together until smooth but not over-mixed.

4   Pour into the prepared tin, easing it into the corners and smoothing the top level. Bake for 18 minutes or until golden and a skewer inserted comes out clean.

5   Allow to cool slightly before transferring to a wire rack. Once completely cold store in an airtight tin. Cut into squares before serving with cups of hot, strong tea.

NELSON CAKE

Also known as Nelson slice or squares, this is like a lighter version of Wet Nellie (see p92) enclosed in pastry. Versions have been made in bakeries for donkey's years: it's a handy way of using up unsold cake at the end of the day. Costing pennies, it was understandably a popular treat for schoolchildren.

Over in Ireland, incidentally, something similar is known as gur cake or Chester cake. Gur, comes from gurrier, a Dublin word for street urchin. Gurs would visit bakeries at the end of the day, hoping for scraps of leftover cake and trimmings.

Use whatever cake you have to hand: plain sponge, jam sponge, ginger and fruit cake all work well.

CUTS INTO 16 SLICES

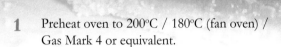

1. Preheat oven to 200°C / 180°C (fan oven) / Gas Mark 4 or equivalent.

2. Make pastry by hand or alternatively, whiz flour and butter into crumbs in a food processor. Add water and whiz until large clumps form. Transfer to an un-floured board and knead gently together.

3. Divide into 2 pieces, one slightly larger than the other. Flour board and rolling pin lightly and roll smaller piece into a rectangle to fit tin. Press lightly into tin, trim edges and prick all over.

4. Combine cake, fruit, spice, tea and rum. Spread over pastry base leaving room to tuck in top layer of pastry.

5. Roll out second rectangle and lay over cake mixture, tucking the sides in gently. Firm to seal and trim.

6. Brush with egg: very lightly score a pattern on top if you like. Dust with sugar and bake for 25 minutes or until golden brown.

7. Cool in tin, transfer to a board, trim edges and cut into squares.

8. Eat warm or cold with a strong cup of tea.

You will need a greased 21cm (8in) square tin, the bottom lined with greaseproof paper

220g (8oz) **plain flour**

110g (4oz) **cold salted butter, diced**

3 tablespoons **cold water**

300g (11oz) **crumbled cake**

125g (5oz) **mixed dried fruit and peel**

2 teaspoons **mixed spice**

150ml (¼ pint) **strong tea**

2 tablespoons **dark rum**

1 **small egg, beaten**

Extra sugar

NOWT CAKE

This is a good little cake when you've got nowt in for unexpected visitors or you just fancy a bit o' summat.

It's based on an original recipe from the 1957 *Yorkshire WI Recipe Book*, subtitled "Through Yorkshire's Kitchen Door". The book notes: "This mixture can be used as the base for a chocolate cake with the addition of one ounce of cocoa, or for a cherry or fruit cake with appropriate additions."

Tips: there's no need to go throwing your money about, but butter gives a better flavour than the original margarine. Granulated sugar is fine but caster is better. Make sure your self-raising flour is fresh.

70g (2½oz) **sugar**	**1** Preheat oven to 180°C / 160°C (fan oven) / Gas Mark 4 or equivalent.
70g (2½oz) **softened butter**	
1 medium–large egg, beaten	**2** You'll need a greased 18cm (7 inch) loose bottomed sandwich tin.
70g (2½oz) **self-raising flour**	**3** Cream sugar and butter and add egg alternately with flour and salt. Add milk and mix well.
Pinch of salt	
2 tablespoons **milk**	**4** Bake for 15 minutes or until a skewer inserted comes out clean.

DOUBLE CHOCOLATE
NOWT CAKE

Here's a more luxurious double-size version of plain nowt cake with some of the flour substituted for cocoa powder. Use a food processor or electric mixer if you prefer. Cuts into 8 slices.

1   Preheat oven to 180°C / 160°C (fan oven) / Gas Mark 4 or equivalent.

2   You will need a greased 20cm (8in) loose-bottomed cake tin lined with greaseproof paper.

3   Line the tin with a 2cm collar 'standing proud'.

4   Cream butter and sugar till light and fluffy. Sift flour, cocoa and raising agents together. Sprinkle some over the mix, then a little egg and the salt. Top with a little more flour and beat together. Repeat with remaining egg and flour in 2 further stages.

5   Beat until smooth and well mixed.

6   Pour into prepared tin and bake for 35 minutes or until a skewer inserted comes out clean.

7   Cool in tin: you will need to pour the icing over whilst the cake is still in the tin.

Cuts into 8 slices

150g (5oz) **butter, softened**

150g (5oz) **golden caster sugar**

125g (5oz) **plain flour**

25g (1oz) **cocoa powder**

1 level teaspoon **bicarbonate of soda**

2 level teaspoons **cream of tartar**

2 **medium large eggs**

Pinch of salt

4 tablespoons **milk**

BOILED CHOCOLATE ICING

This has the most beautiful flavour and smooth texture. It sets almost instantly so spread quickly and then leave it alone or it will smudge. Position any decorations as fast as you can.

110g (4oz) **granulated sugar**

40g (1¾ oz) **salted butter**

40ml (just less than 2 fl oz) **semi-skimmed milk**

90g (3½ oz) **dark chocolate (Bournville strikes exactly the right note for this nostalgic treat)**

1   Combine sugar, butter and milk in a small heavy bottomed saucepan.

2   Bring to the boil, stirring constantly. Boil for 30 seconds stirring all the time.

3   Remove from heat and add chocolate.

4   Stir until melted, then immediately pour over cake and smooth swiftly into place with a flexible spatula.

Note: if you ever need to double up on icing quantities, boil for 1 minute.

OLD WIFE'S CAKE

Popular in Yorkshire in the last century, especially at Christmas, this is so delicious you'll want to make it all year round. It's a biscuit-y shortcake rather than a soft sponge cake and has the most beautiful flavour.

110g (4oz) butter, at room temperature

110g (4oz) golden granulated sugar, plus extra for sprinkling (optional)

110g (4oz) currants (or use raisins)

225g (8oz) plain flour

½ teaspoon bicarbonate of soda

Plenty of grated nutmeg

Generous squeeze of lemon juice

½ tablespoon milk

CUTS INTO 16 SQUARES

1 Preheat oven to 160°C / 140°C (fan oven) / Gas Mark 3 or equivalent.

2 You will need a greased 20cm (8in) brownie tin or baking dish, the bottom lined with greaseproof paper cut to fit.

3 Cream butter and sugar, stir in currants. Combine flour and bicarbonate of soda and stir into mixture. Stir in nutmeg, lemon juice and lastly milk.

4 (Alternatively, for a super-quick version use a food processor. Whiz butter and sugar until creamed and fluffy, whiz in flour, bicarbonate of soda, nutmeg lemon and milk. Remove blade and stir in currants.)

5 Press into tin and smooth top. Try to push as much fruit below the surface as possible as it can become dry and hard in the heat of the oven. Sprinkle with sugar if using. Bake for 25-30 minutes until just turning pale golden on top. Mark into squares.

Special Christmas Editions of Old Wife's Cake

For an extra-special Christmas version, make as above but add a teaspoon or so of mixed spice and swap the currants or raisins for mixed dried fruit and peel.

For a more modern flavour, take out the spice and add the finely grated zest of half a lemon or a small orange and swap the mixed fruit for cranberries.

CUTS INTO 16 SQUARES

PARKIN

Although particularly associated with Bonfire Night, when in Yorkshire, any time is the right time for a piece of moist, dark, sticky, parkin and a cup of tea.

A major part of Guy Fawkes celebrations in the north for generations, parkin was originally made with lard. Margarine and butter have often been substituted in recent decades but butter has the best flavour by far. It's beautiful freshly made and fluffy, but keep it in a tin for a week or two to enjoy the true parkin flavour.

It also goes very well with a glass of milk or ginger wine; sometimes, a dab of butter doesn't go amiss either.

1. Preheat oven to 170oC / 150oC (fan oven) / Gas Mark 3 or equivalent.

2. You will need a greased 20cm (8inch) square baking tin or similar, the bottom lined with greaseproof paper.

3. Heat syrup, treacle, sugar, butter and water together over a moderate heat until the butter has melted and the sugar has lost its grittiness.

4. Set aside for a few moments then very gradually whisk in the oatmeal. Leave for 10 minutes to allow the oatmeal to swell.

5. Sift flour, baking powder and ginger together and whisk half gradually into the cooling mixture. Whisk in the eggs with a little more flour. Whisk in remaining flour.

6. Pour into prepared tin and bake for 30 minutes or until a skewer inserted comes out clean.

7. Cool in the tin. Once cool, wrap in greaseproof paper and foil and store in an airtight container.

See Harcakes (p126) and Yorkshire Moggy (p88) for more detail on parkin's ancient heritage.

2 generous tablespoons **golden syrup**

5 generous household tablespoons **black treacle**

50g (2oz) **soft dark brown sugar**

200g (7oz) **salted butter, diced**

150ml (¼ pint) **cold water**

100g (4oz) **oatmeal, ideally fine ground, otherwise use medium**

250g (9oz) **plain flour**

2½ teaspoons **baking powder**

5 teaspoons **ground ginger**

2 medium eggs, lightly beaten

CUTS INTO 8 WEDGES

YORKSHIRE
APPLE SCONE

This unusual scone is adapted from a recipe collected by former *Dalesman* cookery writer Mrs Appleby, who travelled the length and breadth of the Dales to research her book *Yorkshire Recipes*, published in 1964. Serve warm from the oven with thick cream and an extra sprinkling of sugar.

350g (12oz) **plain flour**	**1** Preheat oven to 220°C / 200°C (fan oven) / Gas Mark 7 or equivalent.
3 level teaspoons **cream of tartar**	**2** You will need a buttered 22cm (9in) pie plate
1½ teaspoons **bicarbonate of soda**	**3** Sieve flour and raising agents into a roomy bowl. Rub in butter to make coarse crumbs. Stir in sugar. Gradually stir in egg and milk to make a soft dough (you may not need it all).
60g (2¼oz) **cold salted butter, diced**	
25g (1oz) **granulated sugar**	**4** Knead gently, divide into 2. Pat and roll into rounds the same size as the pie plate and lay one piece in the bottom.
1 **medium-large beaten egg, made up to** 160ml (5½ fl oz) **with milk**	**5** Grate half apple and slice other half wafer thin. Sprinkle with lemon juice.
Plus:	**6** Spread grated apple over base with most of sugar and cinnamon to taste. Lay sliced apples over and scatter with remaining sugar.
1 **large Bramley apple, peeled and cored**	**7** Lay second dough circle of on top, firming edges gently, Brush with egg and make several slits through the top layer.
Squeeze of lemon juice as required	**8** Bake for 20 minutes, reduce heat to 180C (fan oven)/gas mark 6 and bake 10 minutes more or until golden and a skewer inserted comes out clean.
75g (3oz) **granulated sugar**	
Ground cinnamon to taste	**9** Cool slightly and cut into wedges.
1 **small egg, beaten**	

YORKSHIRE CURD TARTS

Curd tarts are a speciality of the Yorkshire Dales, traditionally made with the fresh curds left over from cheese-making. We had something similar over in Lincoln when I was growing up and it was always in demand from the local baker's. Proper curd cheese is often hard to get hold of now but you can use cottage cheese instead.

MAKES 24 TARTS

160g (6oz) **plain flour**

40g (1½oz) **cold salted butter, diced**

40g (1½oz) **cold lard, diced (or use all butter if you prefer)**

2 tablespoons **cold water**

For the filling:

40g (1½oz) **softened butter**

25g (1oz) **caster sugar**

150g (5oz) **curd cheese if available (or cottage cheese, drain off any whey)**

1 **medium egg**

50g (2oz) **currants**

Grated nutmeg for finishing (optional)

1 Preheat oven to 200°C / 180°C (fan oven) / Gas Mark 6 or equivalent.

2 You will need 2 greased 12-cup tart tins and a 6cm (2½in) fluted cutter.

3 For the pastry: Rub flour and butter into fine crumbs and add water gradually. Knead gently into a ball. Roll out on a lightly floured board to approximate thickness of slightly less than a pound coin. Cut out circles and line tins.

(A food processor makes light work of the pastry: after adding water pulse only until large clumps form. Remove from machine and form gently into a ball.)

4 For the filling: beat butter and sugar together until soft and fluffy and mix in curd cheese, egg and currants.

5 Spoon a rounded teaspoon of filling into each tart case, dust with nutmeg if using, and bake for 15 minutes or until puffed and golden.

6 Cool on a wire rack. Wonderful with a cup of tea.

Tip: make one medium-size tart (use an 18cm/7in tart tin and bake 20-30 minutes) if you prefer. There is also a rectangular version, known as a Yorkshire curd slice.

YORKSHIRE MOGGY

Not a well-loved local Yorkshire breed of cat but fluffy and ginger all the same, moggy is a distant relative of parkin. Lighter in colour and texture, gingery-brown moggy contains no oatmeal.

Stretching back down the centuries, it's thought the name may be from Old Norse *múgi* meaning heap of corn. Like parkin, it was made in late October or early November for the Celtic feast Samhain; later adapting easily to the new Christian festivals of All Saints' and All Souls' Days, All Hallows' Eve, Martinmas and later Guy Fawkes' Night.

CUTS INTO 16 SQUARES

1   Preheat oven to 160°C / 140°C (fan oven) / Gas Mark 2 or equivalent.

2   You will need a greased square 21cm (8 inch) cake tin: the bottom lined with greaseproof paper.

3   Melt butter, syrup, sugar and treacle slowly in a small pan. Stir thoroughly.

4   Sieve flour, raising agents and ginger into a roomy bowl that will fit comfortably into the crook of your arm. Make a well and pour in the syrup mixture.

5   Using a fork, and holding the bowl under your arm, gradually draw the thick syrup mix into the flour.

6   Once as combined as possible, beat egg and milk together and add gradually to the mixture, stirring constantly, until all is incorporated. As the mixture loosens, change to a whisk.

7   Pour into prepared tin and bake for around 40 minutes until golden brown and skewer inserted comes out clean.

8   Cool in tin. You can eat it straight away, fresh, fluffy and already sticky but it keeps well for several days, developing nicely in stickiness and flavour.

50g (2oz) **butter**

4 tablespoons **golden syrup**

2 tablespoons **black treacle**

4 level tablespoons **golden caster**

250g (9oz) **plain flour**

1 level teaspoon **bicarbonate of soda**

2 level teaspoons **cream of tartar**

3 teaspoons **ground ginger**

1 **egg, made up to 200ml (8floz) with milk**

YORKSHIRE SLAB

Rich and dark, Yorkshire slab fruit cake is the mainstay of many a traditional Yorkshire tea table, picnic or packed lunch. Steeped overnight in tea, and after an initial boiling for maximum fruit plumpness, this handy medium-sized version takes barely an hour in the oven.

500g (1lb 2oz) **mixed dried fruit and peel**

150ml (¼ pint) **mashed* tea, hot or cold**

110g (4oz) **soft dark brown sugar**

2 generous tablespoons **black treacle**

1½ teaspoons **mixed spice**

110g (4oz) **salted butter, diced, plus extra for finishing**

225g (8oz) **plain flour**

2 level teaspoons **baking powder**

2 **medium eggs, lightly beaten**

You will need a greased 20cm (8inch) square ceramic or oven-proof glass roasting dish (or use a brownie tin)

1 Steep dried fruit in tea overnight.

2 Line baking dish with a piece of greaseproof paper cut to fit the bottom.

3 Bring sugar, black treacle, spice, butter and steeped fruit and liquid to the boil in a large pan. Simmer gently for five minutes, stirring occasionally. Leave to cool.

4 Preheat oven to 170°C / 150°C (fan oven) / Gas Mark 3 or equivalent.

5 Add baking powder to weighed flour and sieve some over the cooled mixture. Add eggs one at a time topped with a little more flour, fold in each one separately. Fold in remaining flour gradually.

6 Pour into prepared tin, smooth top and bake for approximately 50-60 minutes until springy to the touch and a skewer inserted comes out clean. You may like to cover the cake with foil for the last 15-20 minutes.

7 Brush with melted butter as soon as it comes out of the oven. Leave to cool in the dish before turning out.

8 Store in an airtight tin. Terrific with a wedge of Wensleydale and a cup of strong tea.

*Northern word for brewed in connection with tea, as in "Is that tea mashed yet?"

WET NELLIE

Wet Nellie or Nelly is really just a nice simple moist bread pudding. It's always cut into squares and just as good warm from the oven with custard as it is cold with a cup of tea. It travels well so it's ideal for packed lunches and picnics.

It's similar to another cake called Nelson Cake – possibly not quite as moist and usually sandwiched between two layers of pastry. Whereas Wet Nellie is made with bread, Nelson cake might include scraps of leftover cake as well – or be made entirely from cake.

Both recipes are handy ways of utilising leftovers both at home or in professional bakeries.

Here's a nice big generous tray of Wet Nellie made in a roasting tin: just the job for family get-togethers. A ration of rum is included as a tribute to Lord Nelson.

Alternatively, freeze some: cut into squares, wrapped in greaseproof paper and sealed in freezer bags. It'll keep you going for weeks! Defrost and heat through for 15-20 minutes. See oven temperature below.

Cuts into 20 pieces or more

1 litre (1¾ pints) **milk**

500g (1lb 2oz) **stale bread (brown, white, fruit, anything) crumbled into pieces**

500g (1lb 2oz) **mixed dried fruit & peel**

2 tablespoons **rum (or a spot more, though don't overdo it or you'll have sloshed Nellie!)**

110g (4oz) **dark brown sugar (or slightly less of soft brown or granulated)**

1 tablespoon **mixed spice (or to taste)**

110g (4oz) **melted butter, cooled slightly**

1 medium–large **egg**

1-2 tablespoons **granulated sugar for sprinkling**

1   You will need a greased roasting dish 23x31cm (9x12inches), the bottom lined with greaseproof paper.

2   Preheat oven to 170ºC / 150ºC (fan oven) / Gas Mark 3 or equivalent.

3   Pour milk over bread. Sprinkle rum over fruit, stir and add to bread. Leave for 3-4 hours. Stir in sugar, spice, butter and egg.

4   Pour into dish. Sprinkle top with sugar. Bake for 45 minutes or until golden, bouncy to the touch and a skewer inserted comes out clean.

APPLE DUMPLINGS

When I was a little girl, we had a cookery book at home with a photograph of apple dumplings in it. For some reason, I longed to try them and kept asking my mum to make them. We never actually got round to it in the end and it became a bit of a joke: "And *when* are we going to have apple dumplings?"

Anyway, here they are, after all these years, and very nice they are too. Serve with cream or custard.

SERVES 3

1   Preheat oven to 200°C / 180°C (fan oven) / Gas Mark 6 or equivalent.

2   Make pastry by hand in the usual way.

3   Alternatively, whiz flour and butter into fairly fine crumbs in a food processor. Add sugar, whiz briefly to combine. Add water and whiz until large clumps form. Transfer from processor to an un-floured board and knead gently together.

4   Divide pastry into 3 pieces. Flour board and rolling pin lightly.

5   Peel and core apples.

6   Break off a small piece of pastry from each third and use it to cut out a couple of pastry leaves for each dumpling. Score each leaf with the point of a kitchen knife to represent veins.

7   Roll the pieces of pastry into circles.

8   Position an apple onto each of the pastry circles and fill the cored middles with 1-2 teaspoons of Demerara and top with raisins.

9   Bring the pastry up around each apple to cover it completely, turning and moulding each apple in your hands to seal.

10 Brush with water, stick on leaves, brush leaves with water and sprinkle each dumpling with caster sugar.

11 Refrigerate for 20 minutes whilst the oven heats.

12 Bake for 25-30 minutes or until the pastry is golden and the apples are tender.

260g (9oz) **plain flour**

130g (4½oz) **cold salted butter, diced**

1 tablespoon **caster sugar**

3½ tablespoons **cold water**

Plus:

3 **Bramley apples**

5-6 teaspoons **Demerara sugar**

Approximately 3-4 teaspoons **raisins**

Caster sugar for sprinkling

You will need a baking tray lined with greaseproof or baking paper

BLACKBERRY AND APPLE
COBBLER

What true Yorkshire person doesn't like summat for nowt? Blackberries picked from late summer hedgerows make a glorious, deep purple, fragrant cobbler.

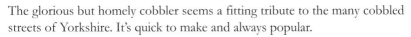

The glorious but homely cobbler seems a fitting tribute to the many cobbled streets of Yorkshire. It's quick to make and always popular.

Not exactly British originally, cobblers were developed by early American settlers. Unable to make their favourite pies and puddings from home without some of the usual ingredients and with only rudimentary cooking equipment, they improvised by laying circles of biscuit dough on top of stews and fruit.

The name 'cobbler' may well come from the way the half-scone, half-biscuit topping looks like cobbles laid over the filling; or it may be the fact it seems to be just hastily 'cobbled together'.

SERVES 4-6

1. Preheat the oven to 200°C / 180°C (fan oven) / Gas Mark 6 or equivalent.

2. You will need a 1-litre capacity baking dish and a baking tray.

3. Peel and core apples. Quarter and slice each quarter into 4. Put in a pan with sugar and apple juice. Simmer until just tender. Gently stir in blackberries for last 3-4 minutes until juices begin to run but berries are still whole.

4. Spoon fruit into baking dish: it should come ¾ of the way to the top. Set the dish on the baking tray (this will prevent any drips of juice spilling over onto the bottom of the oven).

5. Combine flour, baking powder and sugar and stir in melted butter. Working quickly, whilst still warm, take balls of the rich crumbly dough similar in size to a small satsuma and squeeze and shape into flat discs 1cm thick. Lay across the fruit, touching but not overlapping.

6. Bake for 18-20 minutes or until the cobbles are golden and the fruit bubbling.

7. Serve with thick cream or custard.

600g (1¼lbs) **Bramley apples**

200g (7oz) **blackberries**

2 heaped tablespoons **golden caster sugar**

4 tablespoons **apple juice (or water)**

Plus:

250g (9oz) **plain flour**

2 level teaspoons **baking powder**

175g (6oz) **golden caster sugar**

150g (5oz) **salted butter, melted**

Tips

Sprinkle the cobbles with extra sugar before serving.

Make individual 'cobbles' in ramekins with a single, slightly smaller disc of dough. Bake as before.

BROWN BREAD
ICE CREAM

This unlikely sounding ice cream dates back to Victorian times. Originally made in grand country house kitchens, it's a clever way to use up stale bread. My dear old nana worked as a cook in a country house in Yorkshire before she married. I never heard her mention it but whenever I make it I think of her.

A few scraps of dry bread turned into caramelised crumbs miraculously transform plain vanilla ice cream into the most delicious – and surprisingly modern tasting – iced treat. In modern kitchens, kitchen appliances and gadgets take the place of kitchen servants.

Try serving with fresh raspberries: the flavours and textures work together beautifully.

125g (5oz) **dry brown bread (if still fresh, toast lightly and allow to cool) broken into small pieces**

50g (2oz) **soft light brown sugar**

50g (2oz) **butter, melted**

Plus:

4 **large egg yolks**

½ teaspoon **vanilla bean paste**

30g (1½oz) **golden caster sugar**

1 level teaspoon **cornflour**

300ml (½ pint) **milk**

300ml (½ pint) **double cream**

1. Whiz bread, sugar and butter briefly into coarse, lumpy crumbs in a food processor.

2. Spread over a baking tray lined with greaseproof paper and bake in a pre-heated oven at 200°C / 180°C (fan oven) / Gas Mark 6 or equivalent for 15-20 minutes until golden. Set aside to cool.

3. Whisk yolks with vanilla, sugar and cornflour.

4. Heat milk in a heavy-bottomed milk pan until almost but not quite boiling.

5. Pour milk gradually over egg mixture, whisking constantly.

6. Return to washed pan and heat gently, stirring constantly, until mixture thickens enough to coat the back of a spoon.

7. Pour into a non-metallic bowl and gradually whisk in cream.

8. If you have an ice cream machine, follow the maker's instructions. Once the machine has finished, transfer to a lidded freezer box, stir in crumbs and freeze.

9. Otherwise, whisk mixture thoroughly and pour into a lidded freezer box. Freeze for an hour, beat vigorously with a wooden spoon and return to freezer. Repeat after 30 minutes, and again after another 30 minutes. Stir in crumbs and return to freezer.

10. Remove from freezer 20 minutes before serving.

Tip: reserve a few crumbs and scatter over ice cream just before serving.

HAREWOOD HOUSE
MINCEMEAT PUDDING

Based on an old recipe from the kitchens of Harewood House near Leeds in the 1800s, here's a festive steamed version of bread and butter pudding.

It was presented with crème anglaise poured around it on the serving dish but is also good with a more modest cornflour-based custard or cream.

Bake in the oven in a bain-marie for a quicker and simpler alternative to steaming.

SERVES 4

1. You will need a buttered 1-litre (2-pint) pudding basin, the bottom lined with a circle of greaseproof paper, and a shallow baking dish.

2. Spoon an even layer of mincemeat into the bottom of the basin.

3. Dip slices of bread in the 150ml (¼ pint) of milk, gently squeezing out excess.

4. Lay slices of bread evenly over mincemeat. Spread with more mincemeat: repeat layers until within a finger's breadth of the top.

5. Press down gently.

6. Whisk remaining milk with egg and sugar. Prick top of pudding lightly and pour over milk and egg slowly.

7. Leave to stand for an hour or overnight.

8. To bake: cover loosely with greaseproof paper, pleating top to allow for expansion. Tie with string. Stand basin in dish containing an inch or so of warm water.

9. Bake in a preheated oven: 180°C / 160°C (fan oven) / Gas Mark 4 or equivalent for 45-50 minutes or until a skewer inserted comes out virtually clean. Remove greaseproof for final 5-10 minutes for a crisp firm bottom.

10. Loosen edges with a small palette knife. Turn onto serving plate, remove greaseproof disc and decorate with cherries.

2 morning rolls or similar, cut into ½ cm (¼ inch) slices*

150ml (¼ pint) **milk**

500g (1lb) **mincemeat**

1 medium egg, beaten and strained

A further 75ml (2-3 fl oz) **milk**

1 level tablespoon **golden caster sugar**

6-7 **glacé cherries**

The original recipe called for 'stale penny rolls'

HASTY PUDDING

Simple, more-ish and comforting, this is
one of the traditional British puddings
that travelled over to America with the
Pilgrim Fathers.

Once there, it had a bit of a makeover: wheat flour was scarce so early settlers
used cornmeal or 'Indian corn' instead and topped it off with a splash of
newly discovered maple syrup.

Hasty pudding, sometimes known as Indian pudding, is now regarded as an
American classic, whereas the English version has inexplicably fallen out of
favour.

It's is well worth a revival: try both equally delicious versions and see what you
think.

SERVES 4

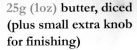

25g (1oz) **butter, diced (plus small extra knob for finishing)**

50g (2oz) **plain flour**

450ml (¾ pint) **milk**

¼ teaspoon **salt (or to taste)**

25g (1oz) **soft brown sugar (plus extra for serving)**

1 **medium–large egg, beaten**

Freshly grated nutmeg

1 Preheat oven to 180°C / 160°C (fan oven) / Gas Mark 4 or equivalent.

2 You will need a buttered 600ml (1 pint) baking dish.

3 Combine butter, flour, milk and sugar in a heavy-bottomed pan. Heat until just boiling, whisking continuously.

4 Remove from heat and whisk in egg. Pour into baking dish, dot with a small amount of butter and grate nutmeg over.

5 Bake for 20 minutes or until golden on top. Serve with a light sprinkling of brown sugar.

American Version

Substitute fine cornmeal or polenta for flour and serve with maple syrup and a dab of butter: you may like to reduce the sugar in the pudding by half.

Some of you may have wistful memories of a flavoured ground pudding called Creamola from years ago. You can't get it now but hasty pudding tastes a lot like it.

PATELEY **FRITTERS**

These delicious puffy fritters are an Ash Wednesday custom well worth reviving. Traditionally served on the Wednesday of Shrovetide in parts of the West Riding, they are equally good eaten fresh and hot sprinkled with sugar, or left to go cold and then lightly toasted and buttered like a pikelet.

This version has been adapted from the two original recipes mentioned in the 1957 version of *The Yorkshire WI Recipe Book*, subtitled "Through Yorkshire's Kitchen Door", contributed by the Nidderdale branch: Pateley itself is a small market town in Nidderdale.

The following quantities make around 10 fritters but it's easy to double quantities for a larger batch.

1. Heat milk until warm to the touch but not scalding.

2. Pour a little in a cup and stir in yeast and sugar. Set aside for a few moments.

3. Add butter to remaining milk to melt.

4. Tip flour, salt and cinnamon into bowl and make well in centre. Stir in milk and yeast and then milk and butter gradually. Change to whisk and mix well until smooth.

5. Stir in dried fruit and apple. For best results and maximum puffiness stand batter in warm place for a couple of until rising and bubbling: this is the yeast getting to work.

6. Melt a little butter in a moderately hot pan and fry 2 tablespoons of batter per fritter: turn over once underside is golden brown. Sprinkle with sugar and eat immediately or toast later.

300ml (½ pint) **milk**

½ teaspoon **easy-bake dried yeast**

2 teaspoons **granulated sugar**

25g (1oz) **butter, finely diced**

150g (5oz) **plain flour**

¼ teaspoon **salt**

¼ teaspoon **cinnamon**

50g (2oz) **mixed dried fruit & peel**

1 **small eating apple peeled & finely diced**

Plus:

Extra butter for frying and sugar for sprinkling

RHUBARB
COBBLER

Famed Yorkshire rhubarb makes a lovely cobbler.

1 Preheat oven to 200°C / 180°C (fan oven) / Gas Mark 6 or equivalent.

2 You will need a 1 litre capacity baking dish & a baking tray.

3 Combine rhubarb and sugar and leave for 20-30 minutes until juices run. Add water and cook gently for 10 minutes or until just tender.

4 Spoon fruit into baking dish: it should come ¾ of the way to the top. Set dish on baking tray (this will prevent any drips of juice spilling over onto the bottom of the oven).

5 Combine flour, baking powder and sugar and stir in melted butter. Working quickly, whilst still warm, take satsuma-size balls of the rich crumbly dough and squeeze and shape into flat discs 1cm thick. Lay over fruit, touching but not overlapping.

6 Bake for 20-25 minutes or until cobbles are golden and fruit bubbling.

7 Sprinkle cobbles with extra sugar before serving with thick cream or custard.

600-700g (1¼lbs) **rhubarb, trimmed, cut into 1 cm (½ inch) pieces**

75g (3oz) **golden caster sugar, or to taste**

1-2 tablespoons **water**

Plus:

250g (9oz) **plain flour**

2 level teaspoons **baking powder**

175g (6oz) **golden caster sugar**

150g (5oz) **salted butter, melted**

SPOTTED **DOG**

Steamed puddings have always been popular in Yorkshire, including this one. Spotted dog is another name for spotted dick. It seems both names for this favourite old nursery steamed pudding come from an early colloquial word for pudding – puddick or puddog – and that absolutely no mischief was intended in the more modern names at all! The spots refer to the dried fruit, usually currants.

This version is made with butter instead of suet – which gives it the most beautiful flavour – and contains eggs and milk instead of plain milk or water. Mixed dried fruit and peel is used in place of currants.

You can steam this pudding in the usual way for 1-1½ hours, but it's easier and quicker to bake it in the oven, plus baking gives the pudding a lovely golden crust on top (or bottom when it's turned out) which makes it even more delicious.

1. Preheat oven to 180°C / 160°C (fan oven) / Gas Mark 4 or equivalent.

2. You will need a buttered 1-litre (2-pint) pudding basin, the bottom lined with a circle of greaseproof paper, and a roasting tin.

3. Sieve flour and raising agents together and rub in butter.

4. Stir in sugar and fruit.

5. Add milk to eggs and stir into dry mix. Blend to a firm dough.

6. Transfer to prepared basin. Smooth top level with a wet tablespoon.

7. Cover loosely with a double thickness of greaseproof paper, pleating the top to allow for expansion. Tie with string.

8. Stand basin in roasting tin containing 2cm warm water.

9. Bake for 45-50 minutes or until a skewer inserted comes out clean.

10. Turn onto a warm serving plate and serve with plenty of custard.

225g (8oz) **plain flour**

1 level teaspoon **bicarbonate of soda**

2 level teaspoons **cream of tartar**

175g (6oz) **mixed dried fruit and peel**

125g (4 ½oz) **salted butter, diced**

50g (2oz) **granulated sugar**

2 **medium eggs, well beaten**

1 tablespoon **milk**

SWEET SUET
PANCAKES

Perfect for Pancake Day, these tasty little morsels may sound unpromisingly stodgy but are unbelievably good, very like a Welsh cake or Singing Hinny in texture. Eat with syrup, jam or honey; a dab of butter is lovely too.

Popular during the last century in Yorkshire, recipes vary: this version contains no sugar in the dough, the sweetness coming from the toppings, but add a small amount of sugar if you prefer.

150g (5oz) **flour**

1 level teaspoon **baking powder**

75g (3oz) **grated butcher's suet or shredded suet from packet**

Pinch salt

1 **small–medium egg**

2 tablespoons **milk**

Pinch salt

Plus:

Butter and / or golden syrup, honey or jam to serve

1 Combine dry ingredients and mix in wet: bring it together with your hands until you have a scone-like dough.

(If you prefer, you can do this in a food processor: process to clumping stage then remove and work gently into dough with your hands).

2 Roll out approximately half an inch (1cm) thick and cut out rounds.

3 Cover bottom of wide pan with oil (or use lard if you prefer) to a depth of ½ an inch and heat to moderately hot. Fry pancakes for around 5 minutes in total until golden brown on both sides.

MAKES 13

TANSY PUDDING

An Easter treat for centuries, tansies originally contained the herb tansy and other greens, intended as a beneficial spring tonic. With plenty of eggs to celebrate Lent's end, they were like a green-tinged omelette.

Gradually, over time, tansies became sweeter and tansy, which turned out to be fairly toxic, was dropped. Other ingredients such as almonds, sweet biscuit or breadcrumbs and orange flower or rose water were included. In some areas fruit tansies, usually made with apples or plums became popular.

Here's a slightly updated tansy, made it the spirit of later sweet ones, it tastes like beautiful egg custard.

SERVES 4-6

For the crumbs:

50g (2oz) **oatcakes, broken into pieces**

20g (³⁄₄oz) **golden granulated sugar**

¼ teaspoon **ground ginger**

20g (³⁄₄oz) **melted butter**

For the tansy:

3 **large eggs**

4 tablespoons **double cream**

Enough whole milk to make up egg/cream quantity to 300ml

¼ teaspoon **orange flower water**

40g (1½oz) **golden caster sugar**

¼ teaspoon **ground ginger**

Similar amount of freshly ground nutmeg

To serve: extra cream and fresh orange slices

1 Preheat oven to 180°C / 160°C (fan oven) / Gas Mark 4 or equivalent.

2 You will need a buttered 23cm (9inch) pie dish or similar and a large roasting tin.

3 Whiz oatcakes into crumbs in a food processor with sugar and ginger. Add butter and whiz until crumbs are evenly coated. Set aside.

4 Whisk 1 egg and 2 yolks with orange flower water and pass through a sieve. Reserve egg whites.

5 Add spices and whisk in sugar gradually. Whisk in milk and cream.

6 Whisk egg whites separately until soft peaks form. Fold gently into egg mixture.

7 Pour into dish and scatter with crumbs. Transfer to roasting tin and pour tepid water halfway up sides.

8 Bake for 20-25 minutes until almost set but still with a slight wobble: it is in effect a delicate egg custard so avoid over-baking.

9 Serve warm or chilled with extra cream and a squeeze of orange juice.

YORKSHIRE MINT PASTY

Unheard of outside parts of Yorkshire, or even in some parts of Yorkshire itself, the mint pasty is a bit of a curiosity. Unlikely as it sounds, the combination of dried fruit, spices and chopped mint is a stunning one: the mint imparting the most beautifully elusive and exotic flavour that's hard to pin down.

Blackcurrant variation

Blackcurrants and mint are another stunning combination: make as opposite but fill with 175g (6oz) blackcurrants, cooked gently in 1-2 tablespoons water, and 1-2 tablespoons granulated sugar until juice starts to run. Strain and add mint as before.

175g (6oz) **currants**

20g (¾oz) **butter**

20g (¾oz) **soft brown sugar**

¾ teaspoon **mixed spice**

1½ tablespoons **water**

Plus:

180g (6oz) **plain flour**

90g (3oz) **cold salted butter, diced**

20g (¾oz) **golden caster sugar, plus more for sprinkling**

2 tablespoons **cold water**

4-6 **small sprigs mint (or to taste)**

1 You will need a greased baking tray.

2 Preheat oven to 200°C / 180°C (fan oven) / Gas Mark 6 or equivalent.

3 Combine filling ingredients. Cook over a medium-high heat for 5 minutes until sugar has melted and liquid reduced. Cool.

4 Rub flour and butter into fine crumbs, stir in sugar and add water gradually. Knead gently into a ball, divide in 4 and roll into discs.

(A food processor makes light work of this: after adding water pulse only until large clumps form. Remove from machine and form gently into a ball.)

5 Chop mint and stir into filling. Divide filling between pasties, fold over, brush edges with water to seal. Indent edges with knife handle or similar, brush pasties with water, sprinkle with sugar and pierce 2 slits with point of knife. Bake for 15-20 minutes until golden.

Tip: use pastry off-cuts to make decorative mint leaves.

BRANDY SNAPS

Brandy snaps were a big favourite at my dear old nana's: I remember delving happily into the white paper bag they always came in whilst she put the kettle on. Dating right back to the Middle Ages, they were popular 'fairings' or sweet treats on sale at fairs up and down the country, and are a favourite at Hull Fair to this day.

There's no actual brandy involved: 'brandy' is more likely to refer to the early waffle or 'branding' irons used to cook them.

They're easy to make at home once you've got the hang of wrapping the baked circles quickly round the greased spoon handles, and they taste exactly like the bought ones.

Bake in batches to allow space to expand and time to roll them all before they harden.

MAKES 18–20

50g (2oz) **salted butter**

50g (2oz) **golden caster sugar**

2 tablespoons **golden syrup**

75g (3oz) **plain flour**

¾ teaspoon **ground ginger (or to taste)**

You will need 2 large baking trays lined with greaseproof paper and several wooden spoons, handles greased with butter

1   Preheat oven to 200ºC / 180ºC (fan oven) / Gas Mark 6 or equivalent.

2   Heat butter, sugar and syrup over a gentle heat until melted and sugar has lost its grittiness.

3   Remove from heat.

4   Sieve flour and ginger together and whisk gradually into butter and syrup mixture.

5   Space heaped teaspoons of mixture onto baking trays.

6   Bake one tray at a time for 5-6 minutes until they turn brandy-snap brown.

7   Cool for 1-2 minutes

8   Using a palette knife to help, ease away from paper and roll onto spoon handles.

9   Wait until almost cold before sliding off handles.

10   Once completely cold store in an airtight tin and eat within a couple of days. Eat as they are or dip both ends in whipped cream.

CINDER TOFFEE

Crispy, chewy and melt in the mouth, all at the same time, golden cinder toffee almost certainly originated in the North of England (its appearance is similar to a burnt-through piece of coal). Traditional across Yorkshire on Guy Fawkes Night, this homespun confection has now spread all round the world, going by various other names such as honeycomb toffee, puff candy, sea foam and hokey pokey.

Easy, if slightly alarming to make, it tastes just like the well-known chocolate-coated commercial version. It's become very trendy in recent years to use crushed cinder toffee to decorate cakes and ice cream.

1   You will need a large heavy-bottomed pan and a 20cm (8in) square cake tin, buttered, with the bottom lined with baking parchment, and a sugar thermometer.

2   Put all the ingredients except the bicarbonate of soda into the pan (there should be enough room for the mixture to expand). Heat gently, stirring constantly until melted and the sugar has lost its grittiness.

3   Turn up heat slightly and bring to the boil. Continue to cook without stirring until bubbling furiously, golden brown and the temperature is 138-142°C (ideally closer to 138°C). This should take 5-10 minutes.

4   Remove from heat immediately and whisk in bicarbonate of soda with a balloon whisk.

5   Pour quickly and smoothly into the tin. Don't touch it: leave to cool and set. Once cold, store wrapped in foil in an airtight tin.

Enough for 10–12 people

325g (11½oz) **golden caster sugar**

60ml (3 tablespoons) **golden syrup**

4 tablespoons **water**

15g (½oz) **butter, diced**

¼ teaspoon **salt**

1 tablespoon **bicarbonate of soda**

FLUFFIN

Although we tend to think of many of our traditional Christmas festive foods as Victorian-inspired, the roots of our favourite recipes stretch much further back: our ancient ancestors also knew how to put on a good spread to cheer up the darkest days of winter.

A popular treat for Anglo-Saxon Yuletides and dating back to the Celts was the rather sweetly named fluffin, a thick and creamy barley porridge eaten on Christmas Eve. A bowl was always offered to the "stranger within the door". Still remembered in the North East, it's also known as Durham barley fluffin. Serves 2.

1   Soak barley in water overnight.

2   Drain barley and simmer with 300ml (½ pint) of the milk, sugar and butter in a heavy bottomed pan.

3   Stir frequently, adding the remaining milk as required and cook for 45 minutes to an hour, until most of the milk is absorbed, the barley is fluffy and tender and the porridge thick and creamy.

4   Serve immediately with nutmeg and brandy.

To reheat: stir in a little more cold milk and cook on the hob until piping hot.

See also Frumenty, page 125

50g (2oz) **pearl barley, soaked overnight in water to cover**

450ml (¾ pint) **milk**

2 level tablespoons **golden granulated sugar**

Knob of salted butter

Plenty of freshly grated nutmeg

Brandy to taste

FRUMENTY
(HOLIDAY VERSION)

Frumenty has been around since Adam was a lad. Originally a plain gruel of cracked wheat, special times of year, such as harvest or Christmas, would see it metamorphose into a gloriously luxurious mix of flavours and textures, enhanced with the best of everything: milk and cream or eggs, spices, dried fruit and alcohol.

Up until the middle of the last century, at least, farmers in Yorkshire and Lincolnshire were still preparing the special version on Christmas morning. It's a custom well worth reviving; simple, nourishing and wholesome, yet very special, try it with a little cream poured over, an extra sprinkling of sugar and a tot of something for Christmas breakfast. Alternatively, you could leave some in a low oven to sustain you on your return from Midnight Mass. It's also a perfect candidate for the slow cooker.

Bulgar or bulgur wheat is similar to cracked wheat but is partially pre-cooked and much easier to use.

Serves 6 approximately

225g (8oz) **bulgar wheat**

110g (4oz) **luxury mixed fruit & peel**

1 tablespoon **golden granulated sugar**

900ml (1½ pints) **milk**

Knob of salted butter

1 Preheat oven to 170°C / 150°C (fan oven) / Gas Mark 3 or equivalent (or preheat a slow cooker*).

2 Heat the milk until almost boiling.

3 Mix bulgur wheat, fruit and sugar together, transfer to baking dish and pour hot milk over.

4 Dot with butter and bake for about an hour until the top is browned and the wheat is soft and has absorbed virtually all the milk.

5 Serve immediately with cream, rum or brandy and a sprinkling of sugar.

*If using a slow cooker, pour in cold milk – increase the amount to 1 litre – and stir in the other ingredients including the knob of butter. Cook on low for 4-6 hours. You can leave it for 6-8 hours but will need to add an extra 150ml (¼ pint) of milk.

HARCAKES

Parkin and harcake are distant cousins. Made from similar ingredients, harcake stayed the original semi-hard biscuit consistency whereas parkin became progressively softer and stickier.

Early versions of the name include thor or tharf cake. They are a harder cake version of parkin. Originally eaten on All Souls' Day, November 2nd, they are also associated with Halloween and Bonfire Night.

Well worth making at any time of year, they taste wonderful and are a good candidate for lunch boxes and picnics. Don't leave out the spices and mixed peel as these are key to the flavour.

Makes at least 24 but easy to halve quantities for a small batch

225g (8oz) **plain flour**

2 level teaspoons **baking powder**

175g (6oz) **salted butter**

225g **Demerara sugar**

225g (8oz) **oatmeal, ideally fine ground, otherwise use medium**

2 teaspoons **ground ginger**

½ teaspoon **ground coriander**

25g (1oz) **mixed peel**

*175g (6oz) **black treacle, warmed**

* *If possible, weigh treacle in saucepan.*

1 Preheat oven to 200°C / 180°C (fan oven) / Gas Mark 6 or equivalent.

2 You will need 2 greased and lined baking trays and a plain round 7cm (3in) cutter.

3 Sift flour, baking powder and spices into a bowl. Rub in butter. Stir in sugar, oatmeal, peel and finally treacle.

4 Transfer to un-floured board, knead gently into a ball.

5 Lightly flour board and roll to between ½ and ¾ cm (¼ in or so) thick with a lightly floured rolling pin. Cut out rounds, transfer to prepared tray and bake for 7-8 minutes.

6 Don't over-bake: the biscuits will still be soft and bendy but harden as they cool. Transfer carefully from tray with fish-slice to a wire rack. They keep well: store in an airtight tin when completely cold.

Note: these are quite different from the fruited soul cakes found in the Midlands and other regions which are softer, paler and richer and marked with a cross on top.

TOM TROT

No Yorkshire Guy Fawkes gathering would be complete without Tom Trot, aka Yorkshire bonfire toffee or plot toffee, which very likely originated in Swaledale. Here's the original recipe.

225g (8oz) **dark brown sugar**

225g (8oz) **black treacle**

110g (4oz) **slightly salted butter**

Simmer ingredients together for half an hour. Drop a teaspoonful into cold water and if it crackles it's ready. Pour into a large greased dish and as soon as cool enough to handle (don't leave it long) work it with the hands, pulling into long lengths and twisting until the toffee looks bright and clear. Break the twists into pieces when cold.

MRS SIMKINS SOFT EATING TOM TROT CARAMELS

I'm a bit of coward when it comes to hard toffee, fearing for everyone's teeth (my own included) so if you're the same, try my easy-to-make and extremely delicious caramel version. You'll be glad you did, honestly!

Makes 36 generous squares

170g (6oz) **salted butter, diced**

100g (4oz) **soft light brown sugar**

3 tablespoons **black treacle**

400ml **tin condensed milk**

1 You will need a square 18cm (8 inch) brownie pan or roasting dish, buttered and lined with greaseproof paper.

2 Combine butter and sugar and stir over medium heat in a deep pan until melted.

3 Stir in treacle and condensed milk.

4 Bring to the boil then decrease to a gentle simmer. Cook for 7-10 minutes, stirring constantly.

5 Once completely smooth and just pulling away from the sides, pour into prepared dish and leave to cool. Cover and refrigerate overnight or for several hours.

6 Mark into squares and wrap in greaseproof paper or similar. Store in fridge or cold larder.

Tips

Fill pan with hot soapy water immediately after use.

Insert lolly sticks to make handy caramel lollies.

Try sprinkling with crushed sea salt flakes for an irresistible modern touch.

Arrange individual squares in paper cake cases: they go down a bomb (no pun intended!) at parties and cake sales.